BASIC THINGS

HOW TO FREE YOURSELF FROM FEELING OVERWHELMED; WHAT YOU DESERVE TO KNOW!

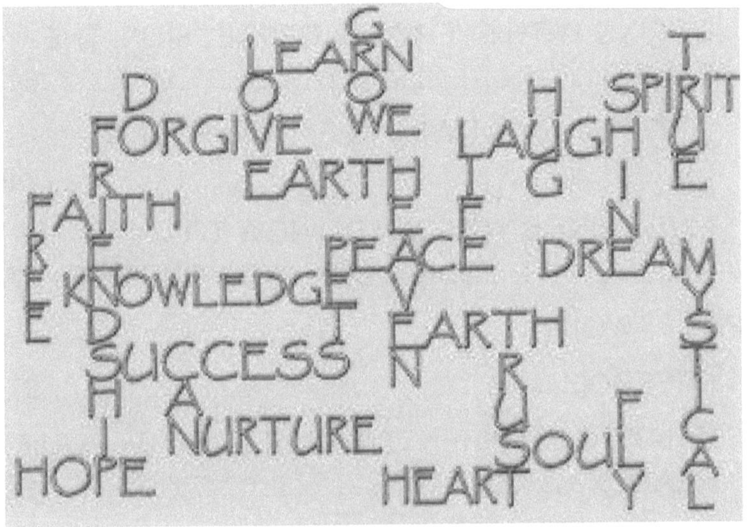

By: Kelly Jones

Table of Contents

INTRODUCTION

Have You Thought About Self Acualization Lately?

Self-actualization is about becoming the best person you can be with the gifts and talents you have been given and midlife and beyond is the perfect time to do this. In most cases you have the time and the money to do it. You have the self-esteem to do it as well and you have the discontent of a repetitive life of pleasuring yourself as a message that life is more than another golf game, another night out with the girls or the latest handbag from that upscale designer you just read about In Style Magazine.

This is the time of sitting quietly with yourself and listening for the call of your soul. Self actualization also means using those gifts and talents for more than simply self indulgence of your every whim and desire, it is to use yourself in service to something with more purpose and mission than your own little king life. I believe we all have something to contribute, whether this is small or grand.

If you want to be a self actualizing person and I hope all who read/listen to this book fall into that category, then the only life to aspire to is the meaningful one. The meaningful life is a self actualizing life and by the way, I say self actualizing as no one is fully self actualized until the move out of this temporal life and into the truly spiritual one beyond this one and even then, who knows, maybe you come back and again and do some more work, as the reincarnation folks believe. But while you are here, I suggest the idea of challenging yourself to be your best self is the only way to go.

If you would like to begin a process of self actualization through power of basic things but don't quite know how to free yourself from feeling overwhelmed and how to get started then, this book is going to discuss that in three parts. I urge you to at least read to the bottom of the first section before you decide that I either can't help you or you are not interested. I especially urge you to keep reading if you would like to be free from feeling overwhelmed.

My goal for this book is to encourage all of you to
diligently motivate, discover and decide what is
holding you from being free and realize your full
potentials.

Stay motivated!!!

BACK TO BASICS 1 - THE MEANING OF LIFE AND OTHER ASSORTED TRIVIA

Over the course of the next few lines I would like to take you on a journey of discovery, one that will hopefully change your life or at least give you the power to look a little deeper into it. For this journey to begin we must at first take a step, not quite a giant leap for mankind but a leap of faith nevertheless. Until you have taken this step your journey cannot begin. Do you believe in a creative force that guides and shapes your life?

The nature and essence of this force at this present stage is irrelevant, it is the belief that matters. Without this belief the journey ends in darkness for that guide is a candle and from it you get light. That's right I'm talking about enlightenment. So this light then, what exactly is it? Basically, to put it in a nutshell it is knowledge, it is what your mind feeds on and from it gets its strength.

Now this knowledge comes over in three strengths, wisdom, spiritual wisdom and loving spiritual wisdom or to put it another way knowledge, knowledge of the divine and divine knowledge. The difference between divine knowledge and knowledge of the divine will be discussed at a later time but at present if you think of knowledge of the divine as knowledge of God's nature and divine knowledge as knowledge of God's essence you will not be too far of track. Without this light you live in darkness and are blind to your true purpose in life, with this light you perceive reality differently for it alters your state of mind. So I guess it must be time for some of this light I have mentioned. What actually is reality?

Reality is a state of mind built on imagination.

Everything around you has been imagined. It has all been designed and so it had to be imagined first. Some by man, the rest has been designed by nature through the medium of evolution.

That is the reality of matter but there is also another reality, the reality of mind. Your perceptions of reality can vary with the emotional mood you are in,in the normal living of life and on another level your perception of life's situations according to your imagined truth. If you perceive a situation in a certain light you behave in a certain manner, imagination builds that state of mind so it is a very potent force. It also works on another level, your imagination of the big picture.

How you perceive what's beyond reality effects how you run your life. If you perceive darkness or death then your lifestyle will be quite materialistic, as a rule of thumb because there are always exceptions, but generally speaking you would be more concerned with looking after yourself in old age and making the most of the short time you've got. With light however you believe that a physical death does not mean a mental death, you don't die you just cast of a shell. Hand in hand with this is a belief in a purpose to life. Whether it is to get to Heaven or have a better new life charitable intent is a main part of both doctrines.

Having established that you live on the next stage of enlightenment is to find out what you are. I have not said who you are as your identity changes with every lifetime. I have said what you are looking for is your essence. To get to your essence takes another step, or leap of faith. That is the belief in reincarnation and here we come to a hurdle for the light has veered off in two directions.

Heaven and Hell or reincarnation. One negates the other for with eternal life in Heaven you only get one life on Earth and with reincarnation you can have many. A bit of conflict but with a little understanding it can be quickly resolved. Up until the fifth century some of the early Christian community believed in reincarnation. When they dropped the belief they took out all the relevant details from the teachings though traces remain. St. Mathew's Gospel, chapter six, talks of a Father in Heaven for everyone in a higher self sort of role and Revelations talks of Jesus coming back under a new name.

Very lateral I'll admit but the belief was well documented anyway so examples are not really necessary. The reasons for this change in direction are unclear to me but whatever they were they were a backward step for they diminished the belief in the soul and enhanced the ego's importance. People who believe in Heaven and Hell believe that their ego's birth was also theirs. They believe that their life started with their birth when in actual reality their life was just another carnation of their soul. This belief diminishes the soul's importance and thus the belief in it.

The soul comes back again and again for like nature it has to evolve to its purpose. The purpose will be revealed at a later stage but at this stage I would just say that you are in essence; an evolving soul on the path of life. Having established that you are an evolving soul on the path of life your next step to enlightenment is to try and find the meaning of life so you might know what it's all about.

***Time is to us as reason needs to be.**

This basically means that we need time to evolve to our purpose and so that was why it was created. The long hand answer is purification of the soul and expansion of the spiritual consciousness to achieve our purpose and be at one with the universe, our purpose being our divinity and the universe our balance. I will take it apart so hopefully you will have more understanding. First, purification of the soul. The soul of an unenlightened person is clouded in darkness and in this darkness there are character flaws. These character flaws are also called demons and as recognition is their downfall I had better list them.

The first one is pride personified by Lucifer, then sloth, Belphegor. gluttony, Beelzebub. envy, Leviathon.avarice, Mammon, lechery, Asmodus and finally anger and Satan. When you recognise them you bring them into the light and so they lose their power over you.

When you know you are angry you are no longer angry kind of thing. Once purified these demons change into arch angels and the sins virtues. Pride becomes humility personified by Gabriel; sloth becomes fortitude personified by Raphael, gluttony temperance personified by Michael, envy hope personified by Uriel, avarice charity personified by Japhiel, lechery faith personified by Zadkiel and anger patience personified by Samael.

With these inside your soul becomes pure as with your nature for your soul transforms it. Hand in hand with this transformation your spiritual consciousness expands for you evolve on two levels, spirit and self. This is done through light and basically you become more conscious of the spiritual world around you, which some call the kingdom of heaven. Spiritual wisdom is the form of light for the spirit expands with knowledge of the divine.

Now having asked you for two leaps of faith it embarrasses' me to have to ask you for a sacrifice. The evolution of both spirit and self is greatly accelerated with the use of a mantra. This mantra must be said seven times in the morning and seven at night. It helps transform your physical will into your spiritual will by cleansing you of your material desire. It goes ' I surrender my will to the greater will, the will of the divine, I will to will thy will'. So to put it in a nutshell your material desire is your ego and it has to be dispensed with before you can obtain your purpose, which is to love.

With every self less act you do whether donate to charity do charitable work or even just open the door for someone for it is the thought that counts, your soul gets stronger and your ego diminishes. So with the light of spiritual wisdom the power of the mantra and love, a selfless act you evolve towards your God head. Now your purpose is your divinity and contrary to popular belief your purpose is to serve and not to be served... You were created to tend the earth on one level and bring tenderness to it on another level.

When you serve, or put someone before yourself you generate an act of love and so activate the law of love which is that you have to give in order to receive. From this activation you receive the Holy Spirit or are transformed by light depending on your doctrine and thus your soul grows in strength. Without an ego you are also more balanced and so are at one with the universe. I had better elaborate on that a little more for it also has a deeper meaning. Within every man there is a universe and balancing it means balancing the elements. I have used the western version of earth, air, water and fire for this to make it easier.

Earth is symbolic of the soul, air the spirit or higher self; water is symbolic of the intellect and fire the imagination. Water and fire make steam, the physical will and fifth element. Now water is very much like the intellect, it goes all over the place and keeps to one level, if its shallow it tends to be quite muddy or clouded by earthly things but I digress. Fire purifies the water by getting rid of the dirt but it also turns it into steam.

To put it another way water is wisdom and fire is the understanding of wisdom in a spiritual sense. Together they make spiritual wisdom or air. The physical will evolves towards the spiritual so disappearing into thoughtlessness and the self evolves to the soul so you lose your self consciousness. When this happens you are in balance for a purified soul is basically in essence a will of light, as above then so below. So a quick recap then. You are here to achieve your God head so you may truly tend the earth. Once the soul has evolved or achieved its God head it becomes an enlightened soul with a purpose to serve. God.

Revelations tells us that there are seven spirits that go to make God. That is the wisdom now here is the understanding. The first one is the spirit of life as symbolised by the outstretched hand of God shooting a lightening bolt into the hand of man. I am afraid I do not know the name of the painting so I cannot give you the wisdom only the understanding. Now the second spirit is the spirit of love, the part of God that is within us all, our creative force.

The third is the spirit of discernment when man knew good from evil and became like Gods. The fourth spirit is the spirit of wisdom your physical will and the fifth your imagination, the spirit of understanding. Basically wisdom is what you know in the sense of knowing the name of the painting and this expands your intellect and understanding is what it actually stands for.

Together these make the sixth spirit; the spirit of knowing so if I knew the name of the painting and understood what it meant it would strengthen this spirit. Now spirit seven is the lord God, the culmination of the mergance of the other six. The spirit of purpose and as it is the lord God it is the purpose that you serve. The seven spirits incidentally tie in with the virtues and sins to make triads. These are the chakras so I guess I had better elaborate, the sins are the negative forces; the virtues are the positive and the spirits the neutrals.

> Pride humility purpose.
> Envy hope knowing.

- ➢ Sloth fortitude wisdom.
- ➢ Lechery faith understanding.
- ➢ Avarice charity insight.
- ➢ Anger patience love.
- ➢ Gluttony temperance life.
- ➢ Blinding isn't it?

Now your next step to enlightenment is to find out how many steps there actually are. We call these the levels of understanding and there are ten of them. On the first step we see the mergance of;two of the spirits. These are the spirits of life and love, a being with the ability to create new life, flora and basic fauna. At the second level we meet the spirit of understanding which at this low level comes over as instinct, so it is a being controlled by its instinct, an animal.

The third level brings us discernment; we know good from evil and can think for ourselves. In hand with this is the spirit of wisdom. We now have both thought and memory and our evolution carries on, on two levels.

Level five is the journey we must go through to purify our souls and grow in wisdom and understanding until we are pure enough to reach level six. This is the mergance of the spirits of wisdom and understanding and it happens when you have an out of body experience in your sleep. Level seven is when your old will dies and is spiritually reborn which is accompanied by level eight when you seem to know all things spiritually.

You are now an enlightened soul you just need a purpose to serve. Level nine, the spirit of purpose and a triad to choose from, love anger or pride. This choice is based on what you imagine God to be, the lord God that is for that's the purpose that you serve. You might choose a God of anger, fire and brimstone kind of thing. You look around the world today and it fills you full of righteous indignation. You might choose a God of pride and thus serve in a self interested way or you might choose a God of love and then move on to the next level for that was the right choice to make. Before we move onto level ten I had better elaborate a little more to try and give you a bigger picture.

If you think of the triad as a three headed dog you won't be far wrong. I have used a dog for it has been conditioned to serve man for the purpose you serve also serves you through the medium of fate. When you are serving your purpose things generally speaking go your way. I say generally speaking for fate only creates the situations. I had better give you an example of this so you can see where I'm coming from.

If you have wrote a book a situation might arise that you meet someone who can help to get it published. Maybe some one who knows a publisher or is a publisher themselves.It is their free will as to whether they act favourably though so it's not a forgone conclusion. If they don't, don't dishearten though for another situation will come along. If it's destined to be then it will happen. Speaking of fate, it is also there to uphold spiritual laws, six to be precise. I have mentioned the law of love earlier so next we have the law of humility, if you take more than you need someone has to go without.

You can see the results all around you so it does not need elaboration. A third law is the law of equality and that says that everyone is equal in the eyes of the lord. We all have this potential for growth within us, we are all evolving souls on the path of life, we are all equal for we are all the same. The law of consequences next, the consequences of one lifetime going into the next and the law of poetic justice next. What you sow so shall you reap and usually in quite an ironic way for the only thing wicked about God is his sense of humour. This is basically the law of consequences in one lifetime. All these five laws are put in place to try and create balance incorporated as a whole in the sixth law, creation regulates itself. And how does this fit in with love, anger and pride?

What you sow so shall you reap. If your God is a destructive God you will live a fairly austere life, personnel tragedies whatever their scale would be seen as punishments for imagined transgressions. If your God is anger you will be fuelled by anger, over riding common sense your perception of divine retribution making you its Nemesis thus generating destruction. What is one life in comparison with the word? Maybe the transgressions were not imagined then. A God of pride would give you a very affluent lifestyle breaking the law of humility. Fuelled by pride you'd think you'd deserved it for progress made and besides you need more than others for you lead a more sophisticated lifestyle being more intelligent thus breaking the law of equality. Fate would be against you but you'd blame any misfortune on other people less enlightened than you so never get the message.

A God of love would give you a balanced lifestyle. Some might consider it austere though you wouldn't for earthly desire would not be a priority. A desire for light and a longing to serve others would be your recompense. So three choices with one thing in common, love. And their relationship to each other, anger comes from righteous indignation or spurned love, pride from self love or misguided love and love straight from the source, divine light. Level ten then, divine light or loving spiritual wisdom. Light at its purest and a deeper understanding of the word.

Every letter becomes another word and so the word becomes a phrase. In this case 'the word' stands for 'spiritual wisdom through love seeing knowing transformation' or to put it another way the knowing transformation is the transformation of wisdom and love in this sense is understanding.

So you get spiritual wisdom through understanding wisdom and this wisdom has another name, it's called the word and there you have it a deeper meaning of 'the word'.

And how do you get to this deeper understanding? You do it through the Hebrew alphabet. Each letter also has a symbol as a meaning. Aleph has an English equivalent of an 'a' with the symbol of an ox. The ox is symbolic of God. Beth 'b' with a house symbolic of self and so forth. Some of the symbols are covered by two letters, hand symbolising blessed has both 'I' and 'y' as does camel symbolic of will with 'c' and 'g'. Before I go any further into the alphabet I had better elaborate more about God's essence and nature.

Think of the grail for it is now within your grasp. The grail was made with a purpose in mind, without that purpose it would not exist. It was made with a purpose and that was to serve. In essence it was made out of gold or spirituality and its nature was one of service or to put it another way an enlightened soul with a purpose to serve. Now the grail written out as a phrase says will knowing God blessed with God's purpose which does not take much imagination to work out.

So back to the alphabet then, I will give you it out in long form and then show you how to understand it. I have used the modern alphabet for we have to move with the times. Incidentally the modern equivalent of the grail would be the Hoover for it is both a noun and a verb saying that its essence and its nature are the same. I have changed G, H and I around so will and spirit turn into spiritual will after blessing and t and u so wisdom and love turn into loving wisdom.

The alphabet.

God's self- will transformed through the word (blessed with spiritual will) blessed with work God's purpose lives (light seeing the word) soul knows understanding loving wisdom (love) loving insight blesses mind.

To refine it you have to take off the supplements For example blessed with spiritual will, once done it reads.

God's self-will transformed through the word. Blessed with work God's purpose lives.

Soul knows- understanding loving wisdom loving insight blesses mind.

Or to put it another way the will is transformed through spiritual wisdom, God's purpose comes to life when you activate it through a selfless act and by understanding spiritual wisdom you get insight into what God actually is. I have bracketed blessed with spiritual will for that is both the evolution and outcome of the transformation, I have also bracketed light seeing the word for light in this case is knowledge of God's purpose which you get from spiritual wisdom. The final bracket is love, which comes after loving spiritual wisdom for that is what loving spiritual wisdom is, pure love.

Easy as a b c

BACK TO BASICS 2 - NUMBERS AND NUMEROUS THINGS

I would like to talk about numbers a while if I may. The universe was built on numbers so hopefully it will build yours. I will be taking you through pure numbers or as some might call them prime numbers. These are numbers divisible by only themselves and the number 1 so I guess I had better start here.

The number 1, what a special number, the purest of the pure. Every number comes from this number just as it goes into every number. Yes it's one on its own. So what is it then? It is the creative force that is within everything that has life, not only pure but simple too. Now from love comes light and understanding, the masculine and feminine forces that are also within us and number two in our blueprint for creation.

These three aspects together become one in the form of a triad. The triad represents the three aspects of the divine, light, love and power. Power in the case of understanding for that is power to your evolution; it is only by understanding things that you grow.

Number five comes next on the list and that is the five states of grace. These are instinct, intellect, spiritual negative and spiritual positive and divine. Basically instinct is controlled by your imagination through emotions and if it was a state of matter it would be solid. Intellect is controlled by the will and would be liquid.

Spiritual negative is when you perceive a God of anger and spiritual positive a God of love. Both these beliefs would come under gas for in essence it is still a spiritual mind. Now the difference between an intellectual mind and a spiritual mind is paralleled in the difference between water and steam. Water travels philosophically in two dimensions, these are time and space. Incidentally if the universe has no end how can it have a beginning but I digress. These dimensions are the dimensions of reality seen and steam rises above that reality into the reality of light. A good an example as any would be the difference between a caterpillar and a butterfly. Do you think that caterpillar believes in butterflies by the way? So anyway, basically it's a deeper level of understanding so when a spiritualist is asked which came first the chicken or the egg he would have to answer neither it was the rooster. Finally we have divine or the fourth state of matter plasma. Its make up is pretty similar to the Great Spirit or collective conscious and still being gas it is also spiritual. If you think of ions or charged particles as enlightened souls and what charges them, electrons, angels or guides. So maybe it was not a bad idea to worship the sun then.

After five comes seven but as we've covered it earlier I will just say the chakras and move onto number eleven. These are the levels of understanding. Previously I said there were 10 levels, which was not strictly true as there are 12. Level 11 is the final cleansing and last step of the journey and 12 is the outcome. The path of light is a strenuous path that brings forth emotional turmoil. This is the soul purging itself of the self's material desires. It has to do this to grow so when you think that fate is against you it might actually be doing you a favour. Don't change into a flagellant though for it doesn't work with physical, only emotional pain. On another level the path of light is mentally speaking very draining so level 11 is actually a time of convalescence when you grow in loving spiritual wisdom. It is a time of study and mental contemplation before you come back to life.

Next number 13, the 13 spiritual gifts. For this one I would like to bring in another strand of esoteric thought and that is Celtic mythology, light is everywhere if you know what to look for. Incidentally the 12 labours of Heracles are also the levels of understanding but I don't want to go too far off track. Now the 13 treasures are the sovereignty bestowing objects and are to be kept by Merlin in his glass house on Bardsey Island.

They only work when used by worthy people or to put it another way they can only be used with good intent and by the fact that they are sovereignty bestowing they are what we'd call spiritual gifts.

Before I go into them I would like to mention the elements and give you the equivalent symbols. For earth we use the grail, fire the spear, water the sword and air the shield. All the gifts come through the elements so I will include them. We use the grail for the soul for that is the purpose you serve, the shield for air for at this stage it is divine protection, one of the gifts. The sword is the intellect for it only fights close up mentally speaking that is, the lance is imagination for it can fight at a distance. Hopefully it will become clearer as I proceed.

Now the first gift was the sword of Rhydderch the Generous and was called Dyrnwyn, when used for noble purpose it would flame from hilt to tip. Think of the sword as the intellect and the fire as imagination so what you have is a balanced (purified) mind. Onto the next gift.

This also comes from the sword, it is the Hamper of Gwyddno Garanhir and whatever food you put into it would return a hundred fold. The food in this case would be the ego and when you lose it you get an access channel to the divine. This goes hand in hand with a balanced mind that's why it came from the sword. The third gift is the Horn of Bran, which dispenses every kind of beverage. It comes from the grail and is the spirit of knowing.

You get this with an access channel to the divine and it comes from the soul for that is what the soul is, the spirit of knowing. Then we come to the Chariot of Morgan the Wealthy, this chariot would take you where ever you want to go at high speed. You just had to think about it and you were there. This comes from the imagination and is actually astral travelling. The fifth gift is the Halter of Clymo Eiddyn. Attach this halter to your bed post and you would catch the horse you desire. It comes from the spear for it is dream interpretation. The horse is a channel to the divine which comes from dreams and to catch it is to understand it. Understanding dreams gives you insight another spirit of God.

Next we have the Knife of Llawfronedd the Horseman; this can carve food for 24 men all at once. It comes from the sword and is the ability to speak on many levels or many tongues if you prefer, carving meat in this case meaning serving wisdom or teaching.

Number seven is the cauldron of Diwrnach the Giant. This would only boil the food of a brave man and comes from the grail. If you think of food uncooked as wisdom then cooked food would be wisdom understood so the cauldron would be a self of understanding. This would be the shift in consciousness after your old self dies.

The eighth treasure is the Whetstone of Tudwal Tudglyd and any brave man who sharpened his sword on it would draw the life out of a person just by wounding him. This comes from the grail and is knowledge of the divine. The life would be replaced by light for the sharpened sword would be a spiritual mind it's more of a teaching thing.

Next we come to is the Coat of Padarn Red-Coat; this would only fit a noble man and comes from the shield so it's a form of protection. A coat is there to protect you from the elements and this is what it does. Divine protection. The next gift comes in two for it is the Crock and Dish of Rhygenydd. These are vessels for serving; the dish being food would be the spirit of wisdom and the crock understanding served by the spirit of love. Together they make the Holy Spirit and this comes from the soul for it comes from within.Number twelve is the Chessboard of Gwenddolan.

The pieces were made of silver and gold representing mental and spiritual decisions for we are all pawns in the game of life. This chessboard could play by itself saying that all the decisions were made without man's interference. It's talking about divine guidance. Finally we have the Mantle of Arthur. Who ever wore it would disappear. Without the ego you have a pure aura and that's what the coat is.

So putting them together we have a balanced mind, access to the divine, a self of knowing, astral travelling, dream interpretation, the ability to speak on many levels, a self of understanding, knowledge of the divine, divine protection, the spirits of wisdom and love or loving wisdom the Holy Spirit, divine guidance and a pure aura.

So number 17 then and we come to Pi or the word blessed. 3.142. To get Pi to number 17 you double the 142 to 284 add it together and then add 3. The reason you double it is because it works on two levels so here goes,

There are three aspects of the divine, love, light and power. Its essence is the spirit of love, its elemental make up, earth the soul and spirit of knowing. Air the spirit and spirit of life. Fire, the imagination and spirit of insight and water the will and spirit of wisdom. The combination of 1, 4 and 2 is seven, the seven spirits of God, five I've just named leaving purpose and understanding, the last two on the list, the power.

Masculine purpose and feminine, understanding. 2Pi R is two people knowing the word so to complete the circle you have to enlighten some one else. While we are on Pi I would like to talk about Phi or the spiritual word blessed. It is 0.618 and it constitutes the six spiritual laws, the collective conscious and the eight natural laws. I have mentioned the spiritual laws before so I will just list them. They are the laws of love, humility, equality, consequences, poetic justice and self- regulation.

The 8 natural laws are:

That each organism is to be adapted to the best of his ability

1. to survive in the habitat that surrounds it
2. to survive in the climatic environment around it
3. to survive in the social climate around it
4. to find its niche in the balance of the eco system
5. to defend itself from the prey's point of view and hunt from the predators

6. to find itself a mate for the perpetuation of the species

7. to give the next generation the best chance of survival that it can.

8. through the medium of evolution to achieve its' purpose.

Phi is also known as the golden division and this is what gives creation its harmony and balance.

19 next and a little confession. previously I implied that the crown chakra was a triad of pride, humility and purpose, the feminine, masculine and spiritual forces when the crown is in actuality just spirit. To explain this I will say that the crown is the spirit of purpose and is only activated after the mergence of the other six. Pride is the spirit without purpose and this disappears when you get a purpose, the physical will becomes spiritual or a will of light. Humility is selflessness so does not actually exist, hence pure spirit. So instead of 777 it is 666 + 1 and this makes 19.

Finally number 23. It's back to the levels of understanding once again but on two levels that merge on the 12 or 11+11+1. The first level I have covered earlier with the evolution of the soul and the next one is the evolution of the soul's purpose, life and love. Earlier I said that love was a triad of love, pride and anger so this number helps you to get rid of your anger and pride. This is done through understanding life and love or knowing thy self and loving thy self.To understand life takes 11 steps. These are levels of spiritual attainment. Think of a book with 11 blank pages and after the attainment of each level a page is filled in.

The first page would say logic is the ultimate in faith. You get to this by realising that anything outside reality is conjecture, logic is the rationalisation of this conjecture. Your faith has a basis and is not blind.

Page 2 without direction you are void. You get to this by realising that you were made for a purpose and that is your direction in life, without this purpose your life is empty.

Page 3 a self that has no purpose is the domain of anger. You would get to this by realising that an empty life is a life of anger.

Page 4 anger is the height of frustration. You would get this by realising that with out purpose your mind gets restless and likely to jump on anything as a purpose. Usually these are wrong ones so the mind gets frustrated and you get angry with yourself.

Page 5 impatience-frustration in despair. You would get to this by realising direction gives you hope so without it you get despair, this leads to frustration and this makes you impatient.

Page 6 anger -impatience at its height. You would get to this by realising that impatience is frustration brought about by lack of purpose and this is what makes you angry.

Page 7 direction is the purpose of life. You would get this by realising that purpose gives you balance and therefore peace of mind. It wipes out original sin when man went against his purpose in the first place and purges the soul thus freeing the God within, your directions ultimate aim.

Page 8 love is the heart beat of life. You would get to this by realising that spiritual love, or grace, builds your understanding and is activated by the law of love. This understanding is heat from the light which is a great comforter as another name for it is inner peace, your soul's life.

Page 9 to know thy self is to look within. You would get to this by realising what you are and understanding your elemental make up and understanding that your ego is just a reflection of the soul and not the soul itself.

Page 10 to look within is to know thy purpose. You would get to this by realising that the purpose is within you and is a state of mind.

Page 11 to know thy self is to know thy purpose. You would get this by realising that your true self is your purpose or the purpose that you serve.

To love thy self would be another book

Page 1 emotional thought is surplus mental energy. You would get to this by realising that emotional thought comes from ignorance and has no purpose so is just surplus mental energy.

Page 2 self consciousness is the domain of pride. You would get to this by realising that self consciousness in its essence is just ignorance of the soul. As the soul is the purpose that you serve it leaves a void. The ego takes it up in the form of pride or self love.

Page 3 pride is the height of vanity. You get to this by realising that pride is just mental vanity.

Page 4 pride is paranoia at its height. You would get to this by realising that a downside to self consciousness is paranoia or having a victim complex instead of a God complex two ends of the ego's spectrum.

Page 5 paranoia is the height of vanity. You would get to this by realising paranoia is just vanity and you are not that special to warrant such attention.

Page 6 vanity is self conscious love. You would get to this by realising vanity in essence is self conscious love.

Page 7 love is the beating of a heart. You would get this by realising spiritual love is soul conscious love. This feeds the soul in the same way vanity feeds the ego.

Page 8 God is love. You get to this by realising that God is a trinity of light or wisdom, power or understanding and love.

Page 9 God exists to serve a purpose. You would get to this by realising that by serving your purpose God comes into being.

Page 10 the purpose of God is the purpose to serve. You would get to this by realising that God is an enlightened soul with a purpose to serve.

Page 11 to love thy self is to love thy God. You would get to this by realising that your purpose is to love thy self through the spirit of purpose, the lord God.

The first book cleanses your essence and the second your nature. They merge together at the twelfth page. To know thy self is to love thy God when God and the word becomes God's word.

Simple as 1,2,3!

BACK TO BASICS 3 - SENSE AND SENSUALITY

For the final part of the triad I would like to talk about sensory awareness and maybe try to discern its relevance in day to day living. It comes over in many forms, well five to be precise, one for each of the senses and gives our lives embellishment for variety is the spice of life. Imagine for a moment that everything looked the same, and tasted the same, what a dull life that would be.

Sensory awareness is one of nature's gifts originally put in place to safeguard our health. It evolved over time as we got more discerning. Smell and taste would be a good example so I will start with these. Firstly smell, originally it was put in place as an aid to hunting prey and a defence against the predator and a means to knowing whether something was edible. Now hand in hand with smell on the second point went taste.

If it smelt wrong and did not taste right you did not eat it. These two senses are pretty much interlinked for if you lose your sense of smell it impairs your sense of taste. That was basic survival and no more. With time though we evolved past basic survival and these senses evolved with us. We no longer used our sense of smell as a hunting aid and so it got less acute over distance though more refined by way of compensation as did our taste for we started to eat a more varied diet with a penchant for seasoning. Basically we got self conscious about our food, invented gluttony and lived off the fat of the land. I had better elaborate on gluttony awhile so you might get a little understanding.

Food as anyone will tell you tastes better when you are hungry and by hungry I don't mean just peckish I mean hungry. Once this hunger is sated you feel full and stop eating for food seems to lose its taste. With gluttony however you do not eat when you are truly hungry you eat because you like the taste. It gives you pleasure to do this so it satisfies your desire and not your need. The original four types of taste were sweet, sour, bitter and salt.

These had their uses for bitter usually meant inedible as there was a good chance it was poisonous. Sour generally meant it had gone off and so was also to be avoided. Sweet told you it was safe and salt being essential to life also had a place. From these four types our sense of taste evolved. We started to blend them together and get different tastes and a more discerning palate.

We hungered for the taste and not the sustenance and thus gluttony came into being. The blending of these different tastes went hand in hand with the blending of the different aromas and so our sense of smell also evolved to help us to define them. The ability to taste comes to us through taste buds situated on the tongue and side of the mouth through the medium of saliva. The saliva starts to dissolve the substance and from this you get the taste. The ability to smell is achieved by special receptors called chemoreceptors found in the lining of the nasal cavity. These can detect chemicals that are either carried in the air or dissolved in water and they transmit to the brain to be decoded and detected as a particular smell.

Next on the list would be touch, well more precisely pain. Another sensory aid put in place so you might not get burned. Our whole body is sensitive to touch, through it we discern temperature and pressure and detect pain. It is a safeguard to our physical health and our well being externally for it lets you know, through the medium of pain, when things are amiss.

Touch can also give pleasure and be very therapeutic. Certain parts of the body react to touch. The base of the feet would be a good example to pursue. Any reflexologist will tell you that at the base of your feet is a map of the body. By manipulating certain parts of the base (the top and toes also have a place) you can administer healing all across the body. When we used to walk bare footed we used to heal ourselves en route for the uneven floor would be our masseur and do a fairly good job in the process. The ability to touch is made possible by specialised sets of receptors located in the skin but also in muscles and other internal areas of the body. These transmit, via different nerve pathways, to the brain to be decoded and detected.

The next sense on the list is the ability to hear, a very useful tool to have when out hunting or being hunted. It is also there to warn of danger, the rattle snake and the buzzing bee would be good examples as with snow-slides, landslides and other dangerous natural phenomenon. Along with the ability to hear you have the ability to make noise. At its most basic a growl or a warning shout but it has evolved to communication. The ability to hear comes to us through receptors, often hairlike, that vibrate in response to sound waves. These are air vibrations with a frequency between 20 Hz and 20,000 Hz. They trigger off an electrical impulse in a sensory nerve which is transmitted to the brain which decodes it and interprets it as sound.The ability to make sound comes from the mouths manipulation of the vocal cords through the medium of breath.

Finally, the ability to see, the most useful sensory gift we have. The ability to discern light into colour is done through light receptors in the retina of the eye. These receptors are called Photoceptors and are pigment containing cells. The pigments undergo chemical changes in light of different wave lengths, which generate electrical impulses that travel to the brain via a sensory optic nerve. There are two types of cells containing these pigments, cones which allow for the colour to be detected and rods which allow for night vision for they are sensitive to dim light though they do not detect colour.

We evolved past basic survival and our understanding got a little more discerning. Where once we could barely grunt we became more articulate. We could express our thoughts and feelings, not only through the voice we could do it through the mediums of sight and sound. We invented art in a bid to stimulate sensory pleasure and add to our newly found sense of awareness. So sensory pleasure next then. What actually is it and where does it come from? To find that out we have to understand a little about the brain so I guess I had better start at the core. The brain stem, our instinctive drive for self and species preservation, these are a set of laws enshrined in our being. I have mentioned them in numbers and numerous things but I will relate them once more. They are that every organism to the best of its ability to,

> Survive in the habitat around it

> Survive in the climatic environment around it

> Survive in the social climate around it

> Find its niche in the balance of the eco system

> Defend itself from a prey's point of view and hunt from a predators

> Find itself a mate for the perpetuation of its species

> Give the next generation the best chance of survival that it can

> Through the medium of evolution to achieve its' purpose.

These laws mould our life and give us our drive. Behind the stem we have the Cerebellum which monitors and corrects body movement and above and in front are the Amygdala, the Hippocampus and the Hypothalmus.

These are glands and sub organs that together with the Limbic Cortex form a protective cowl over the brain stem and comprise our emotional brain. It contains our capacity for pain and pleasure, joy, anger, sex and hunger. Wrapped around the Limbic Cortex and divided into two hemispheres by the Corpus Callosum, a bridge of nerve fibres, is the Cerebal Cortex. It is here we think, remember, learn, dream, fantasize and hallucinate. Sensory pleasure comes from the emotional part of the brain. It is the carrot to the stick of sensory pain. It is the joy of sex in the act of procreation. It is the taste and smell of food when you are hungry.

It is the heightening of sensual awareness activated from the emotional brain in its role as the drive wheel of the survival brain. In much the same way as a laboratory rat it guides you, through the mediums of pleasure and pain, to uphold nature's laws. Within the emotional brain lies the Hypothalmus, the mad scientist, this controls the release of endorphins, along with your body temperature, your sex drive, appetite and thirst and basically your moods and behaviour.

It even controls your deep sleep so you can't hide from it at night. With its assistants the Hippocampus which co ordinates the storage of memory and navigation and the Amygdala which process the emotions it reinforces Mother Nature's will on one hand and makes you aware of your body's needs on the other. The final part of the emotional brain is the Limbic Cortex, on a metaphysical level this is the purpose that you serve, your truth, this fuses the inner individual to the outside world. Basically it is your perceptions of reality on a higher plain and on day to day living. From here you get both joy and sadness but also a sense of purpose.

Now the final part of the brain is the superior brain, the Cerebral Cortex and its bridge the Corpus Callosum. The Cerebral Cortex is divided left and right into two hemispheres. The left is our rational side, analytical, logical and calculative. From here we get our language and our consciousness of self. The right is our emotional side, from here comes art and music and the ability to see the big picture. It sees the forest while the left side sees the trees. It also works slightly differently to the left for it works on imagery, it hears noise and from the noise paints its own picture for every note is a different colour.

The three parts of the brain are the result of evolution and so are built over each other like three concentric circles. The smallest one the basic survival brain is called the Archipallium or reptilian brain, the next, the emotional brain is called the Paleopallium or old mammalian brain and the last. The superior brain is called the Neopallium or new mammalian. There is a lot more to the brain than I have mentioned but hopefully that will give you a very rough guide to sate your left hemisphere.

To get the true understanding you have to take the right hand path for that holds the bigger picture. The survival brain is the first level of understanding. A being with the ability to recreate and the emotional brain is the next step on the evolutionary ladder. It now has some understanding though at this level it is still controlled by its instinct through the mediums of pleasure and pain, joy and fear. This is Man before he evolved and transcended the Earth Mother's control of him.

Man found free will and nature's laws though still buried with in him now had an ego to contend with. You see when Adam ate the apple he got the power of discernment, quite a mixed blessing for with it comes self consciousness and that gives us an ego. Where once man served Mother Nature hc now served this and so developed a few negative emotions along the way. His self centredness said that instead of just surviving in the habitat around him he wanted to excel in it. His dwellings got bigger and more ornate, he got avaricious. Instead of migrating with the seasons he stayed over winter and battened down the hatches, he got slothful.

To survive in the social climate around him he got envious and moved in next door to a fellow called Jones. He still had his reproductive urge to perpetuate the species although it was not confined to when his mate was ready to ovulate, he got lecherous. He still wanted to give his offspring the best chance of survival as this was a matter of pride and anger was there to erupt should he want to defend himself, though with hunting out of fashion it took the form of war warmongering. Instead of trying to fit into the eco system around him he started to take more than he needed and got gluttonous. And that is how the seven deadly sins came to be. He also had the virtues to contend with so his powers of discernment were pretty well served.

I suppose the next question would be what makes us serve a purpose for surely our free will would over ride it. To answer that you will have to understand that man by nature is an emotional animal. By serving a purpose it fills him with love. This is done through the hypothalamus through a thing called pleasure.

You serve this cause because it pleases you to do so, you also get a sense of purpose and that fills a gap in your life thus also giving you a sense of well being. To understand the brain properly might take some time so I suggest you put the kettle on (mine's two sugars) and we'll continue when you are comfortable.Al right? Good. Now see that cup of tea you have by your side. Well er. basically that's it. The water is the basis of its life, the survival brain, the sugar the taste of life, the emotional brain and the tea the colour of life, the superior brain with the milk as the ego.

If that sounds a little simplistic I will take it deeper. Each component goes to make the whole yet is independent in its own right. The water you can drink on its own and though tasteless it will quench your thirst. To the reptilian brain that is all that matters so as an entity it is sated. The emotional brain is slightly more refined, it is at a higher state of awareness and so has some understanding. It is the second circle of the concentric circles and so is an expansion of the first.

It has no colour just a sweeter taste and to the emotional mind with its black and white mentality that means that it's safe. The higher brain is yet another refinement, it sees colour and with it a deeper sense of taste or understanding. It is the third circle and so it is an evolution of the other two. From an evolutionary point of view once you are fully evolved you do not need the ego and so lose it. Your physical will becomes spiritual and you embark on a life of selflessness. At this higher level of existence symbolism comes into play. The whole of this passage could be replaced with the symbol of three concentric circles and you would get the same amount of understanding.

You also get a deeper understanding of the word itself as mentioned in the meaning of life and other assorted trivia. Your mind's eye would see From the spirit seeing life through knowing and a life of God (knowing will through understanding) blessing life (word understood seeing light) you get a self of God (knowing wisdom), God's purpose blessed understanding God and a life of God's will (will blessed through)

Yet you would just see from Homer and Marge Simpson you get Bart, Lisa and Maggie. Now to understand how a mind actually works you have to look at photosynthesis and the humble flower. Its roots are the survival laws and from them it gets its water or its life. The stem is its understanding that grows over time and its leaves its senses that gather in knowledge. With photosynthesis the energy from the sun's light mixed with carbon dioxide(absorbed through the leaves) and water makes carbo hydrates with oxygen as a by-product.

To put it on a mental level understanding wisdom mixed with experience from life is your mind's energy. From this it grows in strength and understanding and gets more aware (more leaves) before coming to fruition. The flowering being an enlightened soul. (The physical will being oxygen grows with photosynthesis symbolic of enlightenment, the energy (heat) from the light is wisdom understood (light being wisdom) and carbon dioxide is the by product of breathing or experience gained through life)

Well that's how it should work but the water might be tainted (or the flower in the shade) and growth occur in a different manner. The soul is basically a transformer on one level and a receiver on another. It receives information and transforms the imagination with this information. This information is not just spiritual it is also sensorial and sensual. The soul can feed of sensual pleasure and from this selfishness can grow. You could end up clinging to the pleasures of the material world to the exclusion of the spiritual will for ones strength is the others weakness. This would be the flower with just a little photosynthesis, stunted growth and a lot of foliage for the soul would make you more sensually aware. One is a spiritual life and the other a materialistic.

Incidentally on the spectrum of light red starts at b on the scales, orange c, yellow d, green e, blue f, indigo g and violet a. so in the words of the great Homer

COPING WITH EVERYDAY DEPRESSION: THE BASICS

When someone comes for counseling and tells me that they are depressed, it is important for me to discern how serious their problem is. So I ask them to describe what they are going through. If their problem sounds like deep, ongoing, clinical depression, I refer them to someone more competent than myself. If their problem is perceived as temporary mild depression, I prepare myself to work with them.

In either case, my first duty is to ask them, "Do you want to get better?" They might be startled and respond, "What?" So I ask again, "Do you really want to get better, to get completely rid of your depression?" I hope they say, "Yes, that's why I am here." But they may hesitate to answer my question. Why would anyone hesitate? Depression is not fun. And, whether mild or serious, most people would want to get rid of depression, right? Not necessarily.

Believe it or not, there are some people who feel good about feeling bad. They might not be conscious of it, but they find some pleasure in feeling down. First of all, depression gets them attention. People around them say, "Oh, you look so down. You poor dear. I feel so sorry for you. It must be awful what you are going through. Tell me all about how difficult your life is." Secondly, depression gets them out of work and relieves them of a lot of responsibility. When they are down and out, other people will not turn to them for assistance. Instead, others say, "Oh, I'll do this task. I can see you aren't up to doing anything right now."

In order to get well, a person must want to get well. I mean really want to get well. They must be determined and be fully committed to do whatever it takes to get well. That means they must be willing to spend whatever time it will take, make whatever effort is necessary, call upon whatever resources are available to them, outlay whatever cash is required and, if they are a person of faith, do constant prayer work in order to get well.

If a hypochondriac comes to a doctor for a cure, but doesn't really want to get well, nothing the doctor advises will work. As a counselor I am willing to do all I can for a counselee. But if the counselee is not totally committed to getting rid of their depression, I ask them not to waste my time. Nothing I do will work for them.

When a person with everyday mild depression says they are committed to getting well, we are off and running. I go into my five starting questions.

1) Do you get enough sleep?

2) Do you eat balanced meals?

3) How much exercise do you do each week?

4) How much do you play?

5) Are you getting enough light?

These questions are so obvious that I am almost embarrassed to ask them. But dealing with these fundamental issues up front often alleviates much of the problem.

1) As long as I can remember, "Doctors say..." that the average person requires eight hours of sleep to be healthy and function properly. Nevertheless, many of us are so busy that we tend to cut back on sleep whenever we can. We try to sneak by with less than eight hours. We justify cutting back on sleep because we have so much work to do.

To motivate ourselves to get enough sleep, it helps to remember that sleep deprivation eventually diminishes the effectiveness of our actions. Our reflexes are not as sharp. We tend to make stupid decisions. We are less alert when driving. We may say silly things that we would not say if we more alert. And sleep deprivation eventually affects our mood. We get cranky and crabby. We feel drained, drowsy and all done in. Guess what the solution is?

"Doctors say..." eight hours, or close to it. That's the first step in combating depression.

2) Eating balanced meals is more in the category of "Mother says..." In my case, it was my mother, father and grandmother. When I was growing up I was a fun-loving kid who just wanted to go outside and play. I didn't want to lose playtime by stopping to eat. Fortunately, my dear mother "forced" me to sit down and eat. And since my grandmother was from the farm, she knew what a balanced meal consisted of, so that knowledge got passed to my mother. I grew up healthy and, with good eating habits, have remained healthy. Thanks, Mum.

I have a popular knowledge about nutrition, but am not qualified to give any in-depth advice. All of us need to read and keep abreast with the latest discoveries about how to stay healthy. A firm commitment to our physical well-being begins with a firm commitment to be informed.

For a rule of thumb: No one puts cheap fuel in a Mercedes. Our body is much more precious than a luxury car. We need to treat our body with utmost loving care. We need to provide it with the highest quality and right amount of nutrition. Our body will give us many years of loving service in return.

3) Doctors, mothers, and just about everyone nowadays will tell you about the importance of exercise. It is good not only for physical health, but also for mood elevation, mental alertness, improved digestion, better sleep, greater energy and a sense of accomplishment. Exercise also contributes to longevity.

My mother is physically healthy and mentally alert well into her sixties, in part because she never drove a car! She walked - to the shop, to the bank, to church, to the bus stop and, when she wanted to go into Liverpool town , she walked six blocks to the train. Did I say Liverpool? For all her time shes lived in Liverpool, so that means she often walked in rain, sleet, snow, and wind. What a lady!

"A vigorous five-mile walk will do more good for an unhappy but otherwise healthy adult than all the medicine and psychology in the world."

-- Dr. Paul Dudley White

Getting motivated for exercise is a challenge for many people. They know exercise is important. But they tell themselves, "I'll do it next week." My advice: find exercise that you enjoy doing. Many people enjoy walking. Others prefer jogging, biking, swimming, golf, etc. One of my earlier forms of exercise was roller-skating. Accompanied by good music, I could skate for hours. Gardening does it for others.

Many people live in cold climates where it is difficult to spend time outdoors much of the year. With no access to a gym, indoor health club, or skating rink, what can they do? Walking around a shopping Mall is a possibility, if a Mall is accessible. Calisthenics is usually possible at home, but for some this is not enjoyable. I recommend music. Play a favorite selection and then dance or "dancercise" to the music.

Another strategy is to pretend you are directing an orchestra. This can be a great upper-body workout. If I were rich enough and had the space I would buy a drum set. Have you ever seen an over-weight drummer? What a happy way to stay fit! The trick is to be creative and find an enjoyable way to work out. Any brisk, rhythmic exercise for at least thirty minutes releases molecules in the brain called endorphins, which quickly work to wipe out anxiety and depression and boost self esteem.

"Above all do not lose your desire to walk. Everyday I walk myself into a state of well-being and walk away from every illness. I have walked myself into my best thoughts, and I know of no thought so burdensome that one cannot walk away from it."

-- Soren Kierkegaard

4) One of the first rules of thumb that we were taught as kids was: "All work and no play make Jack a dull boy." Without play, Jack is not only dull but also depressed. Play has the power to resurrect the child within us and thereby reduce the size of adult problems. Play is a great equalizer, bringing together people of all ages, colors and creeds. Play diminishes our possessiveness of material things, encouraging us to share so that others may join in our play. Play helps us gain perspective. Play is an act of freedom.

"Your mental health will be better if you have lots of fun outside of that office."

-- Dr. William Menninger

"People who cannot find time for recreation are obliged sooner of later to find time for illness."

-- John Wanamaker

Most English don't feel valuable unless they are useful and productive. So we work and work in order to produce and produce. We need to balance work with play. Putting fun and relaxation into our day refreshes our spirits and renews our energy. Play is ultimately productive, for it leads to a healthier and more creative life.

The rules are simple:

I.   Grab your hat.
II. Grab your coat.
III. Leave your worries on our doorstep.
IV. Just direct your feet to the playful side of the street.

"The life without festival is a long road without an inn."

- Democritus (400 B.C.)

5) Finally, light. Growing up in a cold region I know how crabby people can get by the time the month of March rolls around. The result of a long, cold winter is called "cabin fever" or "winter blues". It is estimated that 5% to 10% of our population goes through some form of this. A more serious illness afflicting around 6% of English is called Seasonal Affective disorder, SAD. This is the result of having to spend so much time indoors.

Natural light deprivation leads to depression. Darkness contributes to depression. Because sunlight appears to stimulate the production of melatonin, which influences our mood, proper emotional maintenance involves going outdoors every day. Also, all rooms except our bedroom during sleeping hours should be well lit, with bright colors, cheerful pictures and window curtains opened wide.

Full spectrum lighting, which produces light similar to that of the sun, is recommended.

To sum up: In order to progress from blues to smiles to joy, the first step is:

Commitment

Then we need to take stock and see if we are getting enough:

1. Sleep.

2. Nutrition.

3. Exercise.

4. Play.

5. Light.

These strategies are not only an opening plan for dealing with depression. They are part of the basic foundation for a healthy spiritual life. St. Thomas Aquinas reminds us that "grace builds upon nature." If we neglect the legitimate needs of our human nature, our spiritual efforts will have no foundation to build upon. We will be building on air.

10 THINGS THAT WILL KEEP YOU FROM GIVING UP

We have all been there. That moment when we have tried everything we know to do and still do not feel we have achieved what we set out to do. We have fought the fight and have come against the odds but still we have not reached the goal. The only thing we have left to do is the hardest of all... to quit.

For most success-minded people, the idea of quitting is against all they hold dear, however, that does not stop it from entering our thinking from time to time. I am not talking about those who at the first sign of difficulty through up their arms and just give up. The world is full of people who see quitting as their first option and follow that option often.

You are not a quitter. You see quitting as not an option at all. You believe and quote the words of the great coach, Vince Lombardi, who told us: "Winners never quit and quitters never win." Still, in the secret inner chambers of your heart, there are time when the idea of just giving up and moving on is very enticing.

So what do we need to do to keep the demon of defeat away from our door? What are the keys to staying strong and seeing our goals to completion, no matter how long that takes? I have listed 10 simple and basic things you can do to keep defeat at bay and to achieve the success you see in life.

First, I want to share with you a quote from Winston Churchill's famous 1941 speech to his former boy's school. Many of you have read or heard this quote hundreds of times, however, I want you to write it down and carry it with you. This is a great tool to encourage you and help you stand strong in times of doubt and discouragement. It is also the simple truth of success. This thinking took England to victory over some of the darkest days known to mankind, it can get you to your goal as well.

"Never give in--never, never, never, never, in nothing great or small, large or petty, never give in except to convictions of honor and good sense. Never yield to force; never yield to the apparently overwhelming might of the enemy." - Winston Churchill

1. Know What You Want

Would you head off on holliday and not have a destination in mind. I know that many people dream of just heading out and seeing where they may end up, however, you usually end up where you do not wish to be. Those who are successful know where they are going and why they are going there. In short, they know what they want from life. This knowledge is called having goals.

An American Radio and TV personality and success expert, Earl Nightingale (1921-1989) said, "People with goals succeed because they know where they're going." It is a fact that if you know what you want from life you are likely to achieve it. Those who do not know what they want are wondering aimlessly and never finding what they are looking for.

2. Clear Written Goals

Once you know what it is in life you desire, you need to write it down in clear detail. Those who think they will just remember it do not achieve their goals because the change every day. Your mind is always working. It is never stagnate, therefore it is always changing. Trying to remember a definite goal is almost impossible.

Think of it this way. You are going on that trip. You have a map and you know the city you are going to, however, each time you look at the map, the dot for the city changes its place on the map. Will you ever get to where you are going? Not likely. The same is true for your goals. By writing them down you create a map which you can look at and find it the same every time you need to use it.

3. Belief in Your Mission

Belief is a powerful thing. When we believe in what we are doing and see it as an important mission to achieve, we find the strength and courage needed to do what must be done. One of the ways that Winston Churchill encouraged the English people to fight on during those dark days of the war was to always remind them what they were fighting for. It was for England, their home and country. It was to stop the approaching evil and stand for all that was right, good and free.

Belief gives us the why to what we are doing. When you have a strong enough why, the how will always come. Too many give up because they first look for a "how" to succeed rather than a "why" to succeed. When we believe in what we are doing, we will always find a way to overcome any difficulty that comes our way. English philosopher, John Stuart Mill (1806-1873) said: "One person with a belief is equal to ninety-nine who have only interests."

4. Belief in Yourself

Along with believing in your mission, you must also believe in yourself. It is one thing to know what needs to be done, and another to believe that you can do it. I have always found strength in time of struggle by repeating to myself this fact: If I was created with a purpose to complete, then all intentions are for me to complete it. If the Creator of the universe is behind you, how can you fail?

Do not get the belief in yourself confused with conceit. Believing that you can achieve your goals is not believing that you are better than others, only that you can do what you were created to do. Believing in yourself is where we find strength to go that bit farther down the road to achievement. Nineteenth century activist and writer, Lydia M. Child (1802-1880) put it this way, "Belief in oneself is one of the most important bricks in building any successful venture."

5. Passion

Passion is a fire that burns deep in the soul of the one who has a dream. Success-minded people know what their passion to achieve their dreams is the energy that keeps them going when everything seems to tell them to stop. It is that burning desire that fuels the achiever to try just one more thing, take one more step and never to give up.

Like all fires however, passion must be fed. This is where having that written goal come in. Each time it is read it fuels the fires of your passion and helps you to move on. Know that this is not just a wish for success. Wishes are made of smoke and you cannot hold on to them. This is your dream. It is solid, it is real and it is yours.

6. Sense of Adventure

Real success-minded people know that every difficulty, every road block, every challenge is not something to avoid but a new adventure to be embraced. American author, William Feathers

(1889-1981) said, "One way to get the most out of life is to look upon it as an adventure." Adventure give us purpose. It makes the challenges of life exciting. It makes the journey to achievement fun.

The time when we want to give up and quit are the time we feel discouraged, tired and worn-out. When we develop a sense of adventure we start to see those times are something to overcome, not give into. We find the energy to press on and move toward the next great adventure life holds for us.

7. Helping Others

One of the most positive and successful people I have known in my lifetime has been the great author and speaker, Zig Ziglar. I do not believe that any person has inspired me more than Zig to keep going, even when I really, really, really did not want to. What was the key to Zig Ziglar's success and that he passed on to everyone who desires to achieve success? Simple: Help other people.

"You can have anything in life you want," Zig use to say, "as long as you help enough people get what they want." This is one of my favorite quotes of all time. That is because it is 100% true. I have in written down so I can read it often and never forget that success comes from helping others to succeed. By helping others to be their best, you in turn become your best. When it comes to helping others, there is no down side.

8. Purposeful Action

Here is a truth that I want you to write out and attach to your bathroom mirror so you see it every day. Learn it, believe it and never forget it for a moment. It is the foundation to all success in every area of your life. Without it you will never achieve your dreams and with it you will never fail. Ready? Here it is: NOTHING HAPPENS WITHOUT ACTION!

No matter what you want to achieve in life, nothing will be achieved without taking action. You can always do something that you did not do before. It does not matter what you know, who you know or when you know it. Knowledge by itself is incomplete. As the great motivator, Tony Robbins said, "You see, in life, lots of people know what to do, but few people actually do what they know. Knowing is not enough! You must take action."

9. Determination

The way to avoid giving up is to never stop. There is always one more thing you can try. There is always one more turn in the road. Remember the words of the great inventor, Thomas A. Edison (1847-1931) who said, "Our greatest weakness lies in giving up. The most certain way to succeed is always to try just one more time." And Edison knew about trying and failing. Most men would have never moved beyond the many failures that Edison did. But then, we would not have most of the wonderful conveniences we have today without those who were determined to find the answers they sought.

Here is the key to the success of Edison and those many men and women like him who tried and failed over and over again. The key is they never see failure as failure. Just because something did not work does not mean it is a failure. You just discovered something you weren't looking for. As Edison said, "Just because something doesn't do what you planned it to do doesn't mean it's useless."

10. Success

Success is a two-edged sword. There is little in this world as satisfying as success. To know that your hard work and determination paid off and you have won the prize is a great feeling. It is encouraging and exhilarating. However, it can also be the first step to your biggest failure. Few have seen success to the degree that Microsoft founder Bill Gates has. Gates makes this observation about success: "Success is a lousy teacher. It seduces smart people into thinking they can't lose."

Far too many people achieve success in an area of life and then quit. They think that their success will be enough or it will linger in their life. The truth is, success melts like ice cream in the hot sun. It is there and it is wonderful, but if you stop and hold it in your hand you will end up with only a messy hand. The best way to celebrate success of a goal is to immediately set a new goal. Once you have done that, go back to step one and start the adventure all over again.

FIVE THINGS YOU CAN DO NOW TO REJUVENATE YOUR WORK AND YOUR LIFE

If you are in your second act, which can be anytime after forty or between late 20s to 30s, you may find yourself in a place of dissatisfaction, restlessness or fear that you have done what you can do and now it's just a matter of hanging on to what you've accomplished and hoping for the best.

You may feel the next generation of young Turks lining up behind you ready to take over the minute you give them half a chance. Or you could be in a job that you no longer love or one that is threatened by layoffs, downsizing and all manner of other insecurity producing thoughts and feelings. In fact, you may already be out of work due to one of these situations. You may worry about your age, your graying hair and that your skill set may no longer be valid or that the new technology in your field is too daunting for you to learn at this stage of the game.

Well, none of this is true - except for those young Turks, they will always be there, but even they can be brought into your fold if you know how - and the rest you can certainly do something about. I have identified five things that can help you rejuvenate this time in your life. One of the things I know from working with people at midlife and beyond on rejuvenating their lives is that life rewards action - new action - not the same old same old. The other thing I know and I know this with all my heart and soul, - plus there is scientific proof of this - is that your mind and the thoughts you have about yourself on a day by day basis, on a minute by minute basis is the most powerful tool you have to use in creating the life you want, regardless of what that is.

In fact, it's these two things - taking new action and reprogramming your mindset, that separate the winners from the losers in the game of rejuvenating yourself at midlife and beyond. Below are five basic things you can do today to get the ball rolling in the direction of a new and rejuvenated life and work.

1. ***Do something new today:*** If you are employed then look at your work situation, your company, your co-workers, the field it is in and see what is new, what is dying and come up with a new idea to shake things up. Remember the life/death/life cycle of everything organic. Companies and organizations are no different so look at what is dying and stay away from that, even if this is your comfort zone. Look at what is exhibiting new life and go toward that. Volunteer to get involved in the new thing. Take a class on it, at work or on your own time and money - invest in the future of something in your work setting, even if you have to pay for it out of your own pocket. If you are not sure what to do today that is new, then research your field and see what is emerging and go toward that. People who take initiative are the ones who stayed employed.

2. ***Learn something new:*** this does not have to be work related since learning and growing in

any area of your life will have benefits in all areas. When we learn something new it stirs up the neurons in our brains and brings us into the part of our brains that engender growth and this has a positive affect on all aspects of life by putting us into a more receptive place of problem solving. It creates new neural pathways and this in turn generates a lighting up of all our neural pathways. This is why some have said that to keep your brain in good working order you must be learning new things and solving problems your whole life. Learning also increases the serotonin - the feel good brain chemical - in the brain and makes you a happier person and happy, positive, upbeat people are the ones others want to be around and when the time comes to make a layoff, these happy, productive folks will be less likely to get that pink slip.

3. ***Help someone else out by giving and sharing your gifts and talents:*** Instead of fearing those young Turks, take one on and

mentor him or her. These younger folks will be there anyway and if you share what you know and help them then they will be less likely to try to unseat you or take your job in some let's get rid of this old coot sort of way. But be genuine about it - self-serving mentoring will bite you in the butt - no question about it. If mentoring is not your thing, then do something helpful and generous in some other setting. Just as learning something new beings other benefits, so does helping others - it makes you feel good and this increase in good will and positive action increases your serotonin levels again and this too will reap benefits throughout your life and work.

4. *Have faith not hope:* When we have faith we know in our hearts that even though things may be hard at the moment, and I am not denying this to be the case for some of you, but that in spite of this you feel certain that in the long run things will work out for you. When you say you hope something will be

okay down the road, this implies doubt - the very fact that you hope it, means you are not totally sure. So listen for the word hope in your vocabulary and get rid of it. Hope is also innocent and nave. Faith instead is based on knowing and this knowing is based on past experience. By the way, I am not talking about religious faith - that is another story and not what I am talking about here. I am talking about the faith you have in your abilities and in knowing that you can meet the current challenges and come out a winner in the future. This brings us the last thing on my list of five things you can do to rejuvenate your life and work.

5. ***Change Your Self-Talk from Neutral or Negative to Positive:*** In his best- selling book, Learned Optimism, Martin Seligman tells us that, "Life inflicts the same setbacks and tragedies on the optimist as on the pessimist, but the optimist weathers them better...the optimist bounces back from defeat, and, with his life somewhat poorer, he

picks up the pieces and starts again." As he goes on to say, that's the good news - the bad news is that if you are pessimistic then life gets worse and worse by the day. It is a self-fulfilling prophecy. If you think life is noting but trouble and strife, then guess what that is exactly the way it will be for you. I work with people and some are looking for new careers or jobs and they will begin every conversation with me about something they read in the paper or saw on television about the economy and how bad it is. Or about the job search and how the new technology has made it more difficult since there are so many more people able to access the job boards and so on. What these people do is look for the bad news so they can reinforce their already pessimistic view of things. Well, this makes them feel good for about two seconds since it verifies what they were already thinking but it does not serve them in the long run at all.

Here's an exercise you can do to see if you are a negative thinker. Take you average day and divide it into four parts - morning, noon, afternoon and evening. Write down what your basic thoughts are during this time. Don't think about whether you are being positive or negative - just write down your thoughts. Do this for three different days - make one a work day, one a day on the weekend and one a day when you had something to do that was out of the ordinary like a dentist appointment, taking the car into for repairs, that kind of thing.

Now go through and yellow highlight the neutral thoughts - those not positive or particularly negative, then red highlight the really negative ones and then using a green marker highlight the positive thoughts. The ratio you want is three positive to one negative. By the way, yellow is negative and needs to be counted on the negative side of things since it does not increase your optimism. Now for the next 90 days, begin a process of increasing your positive thoughts and decreasing your negative ones by paying attention to the automatic thoughts - particularly the negative ones and making a concentrated effort to rid yourself of them - you'll be surprised at how energizing this can be.

6. A Bonus Idea: Align with others who value who they are and who you are. When it comes to rejuvenating your life being around others who are positive and life affirming about you and about themselves can be one of the most empowering things you can do. They say that you are the average of the five people you spend the most time with so make sure these five people are winners and not losers at the game of life. Like the pessimist who gets a little kick out of being right when he or she points out something negative, being around negative people can feel good in the moment too - it's the old pity party idea. People often bond via their pain and dysfunction, but this just keeps you dysfunctional like them. So find others who want to rejuvenate their lives and start hanging around with them and begin today to move away from those that just want to bitch and moan. Plus, when you do the five things above you'll be too busy to join in the

pity party and will instead be living a rejuvenated life - I guarantee it.

PART TWO

FREEDOM

Why Have You Been Feeling Distracted Lately?

...And is this related to the planetary activations?

Could there be a connection between the spiritual planetary activations and a feeling of being distracted? Have you been noticing that it can seem more difficult to focus, more challenging to feel connected or motivated, or have you simply been aware of a generalized feeling of mild confusion, disconnection, or disinterest? When you look at the deeper energy shift that is happening, and recognize how it can affect your consciousness, the reasons for these symptoms become clearer.

When you clairvoyantly explore the trends in the planet's energy, the underlying planetary vibration can seem to have a dream-like or fantasy quality.

The swirling, shifting energies make everything seem less dense, and there is much more space within everything and everyone. Now this doesn't mean that everyone will see their world this way, and in fact, many people won't. However, the consciousness shifts can certainly make everything feel very different, even if you don't quite have the words to explain it.

Consciousness activation sounds wonderful at first, until you realize that you are acclimated to the familiar, slower paced, more stable feeling of the past. When everything was slower and denser, there was less confusion and more certainty. Whether the things everyone was so certain about were actually grounded in deeper truth is debatable, but it was certainly easier to feel more secure about your identity, and about the stability of the reality around you.

So what happens when your consciousness, and the energy that forms your world, expands into an energetic reality that is less dense? What does it feel like when you notice the moment-by-moment subtle shifting that is characteristic of consciousness itself?

Consciousness shifts instantaneously, and that can be a wonderful thing, if you're ready for it. However, there are many levels of your consciousness that are still living in the world that you remember from the past, because even in the relatively recent past, everything was slower and denser. And that begins to explain the feeling of being distracted...

When the denser world was more stable, you could take the time you needed to comprehend it. Now the feeling is as if the world beneath your feet is shifting. Even the space between your thoughts is shifting. But how do you address this? Do you have to learn entirely new skills of awareness?

You don't have to learn entirely new skills, but you do need to make greater use of the consciousness skills that you have begun to develop. You especially benefit when you cultivate your focus, your patience, your centering, and your ability to shift and release energy. Not that the universe is subjecting you to a test. The universe is not trying to test you, to harass you, or to make you do anything in particular.

The universe is awakening spiritually, and you, being an important element of that very same universe, are awakening spiritually as well. So if you're becoming more aware in your consciousness, and if that is something that you have co-created, why would you be distracted? Shouldn't increased awareness make you more focused and centered?

Why is your need to practice mindfulness in each moment greater than ever before? Remember, it's not because you're being tested, but the challenges result from your being in a world that is now responding to the subtle shifts of consciousness much more quickly. This means that there is a feeling that everything, even your own body and mind, are shifting in each moment.

This feeling is real, because the shifts are actually happening. But just because there are ever present subtle shifts, this doesn't have to lead to the distracted state. And yet, until you recognize that the shifts are happening, and become familiar with them, your logical mind will attempt to track reality at the speed of the past. This is what leads to the distracted feeling.

Your logical mind is trying to make sense of an expanding spectrum of vibrations that is manifesting within all levels of this world. This expansion can more easily be understood with the higher functions of your intuitive heart and your intuitive mind. However, your logical mind can not string together the parts of the shifting energies. It would be like your trying to understand a jig-saw puzzle, if those puzzle pieces were strewn on the floor.

Only the higher aspects of the self can comprehend what the jig-saw puzzle is really about. And as you listen to the wisdom within, you find that at that deep inner level, the jig-saw puzzle has already been put together, though perhaps in a new creative way.

If the world is not going to stand still in the slow and dense way that it did before, how can you remain centered amidst this shift? Even though the shifts are escalating, bringing about changes within you, and all around you, there is a timeless stable reality available for you as well. It has always been there. This is the inner world of your divine timeless soul.

This is a bit of a mystery for many people, because they are very referenced to their logical mind's overwhelmed state. This makes them forget their timeless inner soul's presence. Or perhaps they have only rarely accessed their soul's deeper wisdom. This puts them at a disadvantage in making sense of the shifting energies.

Even in the midst of planetary expansion and awakening, you can always choose to sense your world through the lens of your cosmic soul presence. And when you do that, you start to realize how much everything has energetically shifted.

And yet, this realization that the world -- and everyone in it -- has already significantly shifted energetically, may be too confronting for many people. And so they feel distracted and overwhelmed, but they are not yet able or willing to recognize what is happening to the underlying energetic structure of their body, mind, and soul.

Here are some ways that you can approach the consciousness shifts with ease and grace...

When you feel distracted, disconnected, bored, dull, or overwhelmed, you are probably reacting to the world around you. The world around you was never really the ultimate source of interest and enjoyment for you, though you may have been taught that it was. That is what you thought in the past, because you had not cultivated your deep soul reference point. You didn't realize that the fascination and focus is within you.

So now, with the consciousness shifts, you begin to sense that the world is what it is; the outer world can not make you interested, and it can not make you fascinated or focused. But there is hope, because if you, yourself, could be more spiritually integrated, the world would be so much more fascinating and meaningful to you. A paradox, but what are you to do?

Bring your attention within.

Now this brings up the two aspects of your self that are vital for your success in this adventure:

1. There is that part of you that is actively participating in this process as you read these words, and that part is the conscious mind.

2. Then, there is the deeper level of awareness deep within you, and that part has been known as the sub-conscious self, the super-conscious self, the soul, and at the deepest levels, the higher self.

And all these deeper parts of you need to be united with your conscious mind, because there is a wonderful symbiotic relationship between the conscious self and the deeper aspects of your self.

Your deeper cosmic aspects have the brilliant capacities that allow you to unite all the shifting realities in a centered way, because the deeper levels of self contain all the potentials of the universe within you. A bit astounding to consider, but please let yourself indulge in this possibility for a moment.

When the conscious mind is unaware of the inner potentials of the deep self, the conscious mind can become overly influenced by the shifting energies all around you, without understanding the deeper meaning of everything that is happening in your world. And although the deeper soul wisdom within you understands much, there is little that the deeper self can do without the conscious mind to co-create with it. What is the solution?

The spiritual relationship between your conscious mind and your deeper soul essence helps you access what you need, in each moment, so that you can negotiate the planetary shifts with ease and grace.

Begin to notice your inner self as an energy presence.

Let yourself see and feel it however you choose to - - just use your imagination. Sense the flow between your conscious self and the inner soul presence. It's OK if at first you believe that you're just making it up. That's how you learn. But what do you do if you sense within yourself, and you notice only distraction, confusion, or dullness?

These layers of distraction will shift and release when you bring them to your awareness, in a non-judgmental way. Feel the flow between your conscious mind and your inner self. As you do this, the unconscious energies that have been trapped will start to shift, to move, and eventually to release from your body and aura.

As you continue to explore, you will find that you can access the deeper layers of your radiant soul within. You can activate this process by imagining the light of your soul shining forth from deep within you, so that your soul lights your aura and your environment. And this experience may lead to a realization...

When you begin to reference your inner soul energy, you begin to recognize that the planetary shifts are less confusing, and actually make sense. This is because any structure that has not been centered in a deeper truth is shifting, so that it can rebuild itself based on a deeper cosmic core of truth. For example, certain aspects of the banking industry have been based upon deception, and thus have been disconnected from a deeper reality.

This is not to say that banks are bad, but that they have been generally ungrounded, being disconnected from a deeper spiritual core or truth. And so, as the consciousness shifts happen, banks will evolve and change in a healthy direction. And this means that the world is not disintegrating, because it is actually shifting into alignment with a deeper cosmic reality. The empowering message here is that the deeper reality is easily accessed within your very own self, and it is always there for you in each moment.

+ When you want to know what is real, go within to your soul essence.

+ When you want to know where the fascination and delight is, go within.

+ When you want to know where you can be comforted, assisted, guided, and given the deep sense of alignment that you know you need, go within.

+ When you look around you, and find yourself feeling stuck, overwhelmed, or bored, quietly go within, integrate with the presence there, and look at your world again with a deeper knowing.

Feel the flow between your conscious self and your inner cosmic light. This is your primary relationship. It will always be there for you, amidst all shifting realities.

And when you look at the world, and you recognize that much of it is not grounded in a deeper reality, you will not be dismayed. You will not be distracted or confused. You will just see it, without judgment, and you will recognize what it is.

In the same moment that you recognize what is happening in much of the outer world, you will also recognize, by its contrast, that the deeper level of soul essence, which is known when you engage with your inner cosmic self, is quietly providing you with the inner voice of truth. This is the voice that frees you from confusion, and lets you make empowering choices, and supports you in following those choices as you move forward, guided by your inner cosmic soul, each day.

This inner knowing may be a voice, a feeling, a light, or a generalized, yet quite meaningful sense that you just somehow know that you know. It is real. It is there for you, within.

These aspects of you, in conversation together, can help to co-create the world you seek, in ways great and small, each moment of every day. And your co-creative resonance within naturally harmonizes with other appropriate people, who appear in your reality to further co-create this awakening world.

I thank you for incarnating as the self that you are, so that you could experience these realizations in this moment. And I thank you for igniting the deeper radiance within your self, because even as you read these words, your divine integrated presence is uplifting the world in a wondrously subtle, and yet quite tangible way.

WHAT TO DO WHEN OVERWHELMED BY YOUR REALITY?

At times, life feels like an overwhelming affair. There's too much to do, too much to think, too much to worry about. What can we do to fight that feeling?

Sometimes life seems to be too much to bear. Some people feel overwhelmed by the constant rush and the many things to do. Others just can't stand the incessant murmur of their never-ending thoughts. Some, still, can't cope with their feelings of inadequacy or insecurity. They all try different solutions, among which maybe meditation or mindfulness could be tested, but that is often just not enough to counteract the feeling.

Let us go over some of the causes of such feelings, first, to then study some possible tools and solutions.

I. **Too many things to do:** most of us have grown up in societies in which competition and success are paramount and the true measure of our value. As a consequence, we feel obliged to constantly aim at greater, higher goals. Being good is never enough, as excellence and supremacy are the only acceptable levels. This type of belief, inherited from our environment, pushes us to constantly seek more, do more, expect more of ourselves. There's a whole world to impress in front of us and that demands that we devote most of our time to doing things that will get us closer to our goal and that any free time we happen to find, we also use pursuing our constant improvement.

II. **Too many thoughts:** rumination starts in most human beings as a form of daydreaming. Already in childhood, some people devote quite a lot of their time to letting themselves get lost in their thoughts while disconnecting from reality. What soon becomes a habit is almost invariably paired with negative projections of that future, as we learn to worry about what may be or what may happen. Very few people ruminate about positive, happy things; most do about negative, worrisome or painful ones. Constant thinking about negative aspects quickly becomes a way of life and those who embark on it find it difficult to change the pattern. Any form of rumination, be it focused on the past or the future, yields certain chemicals and sensations that our brain soon becomes addicted to. Not having them can cause withdrawal-like symptoms and result in a permanent need to recreate them. Thus, the rumination continues, grows and becomes never-ending.

III. **Living in the past:** when human beings ruminate, they usually do so focused on two different scenarios, and only those two: the past or the future. When in the past, they are trying to make sense of something that happened that still makes them feel guilty, sad or hurt. Not being able to change whatever happened then often overwhelms them and makes them feel powerless.

115

IV. **Living in the future:** when in the future, people are trying to ready themselves to face something that scares them, constantly asking themselves, 'what if... ?' The more time they spend in those scenarios, the more often they need to return. People who spend so long in the future in their minds become overwhelmed by the wide range of possible difficulties and hurdles they may encounter and by the growing belief in their failure to succeed.

Feeling inadequate or insecure: many people suffer from low self-esteem or insecurities which are the result of weak beliefs and convictions. When a person holds strong beliefs, there is no insecurity. It comes from uncertainty and doubt. Those who feel like they're not good enough or insufficient, tend to find it hard to cope with their circumstances and the reality around them, not because it is posing them too many challenges but because they think they are not capable or strong enough. Everything becomes complicated and one problem piles on top of the next until people feel completely overwhelmed.

So, what can be done?

First of all, take a deep breath. Nothing will change if you can't stop for a second and focus on the task at hand. The more unfocused you are, the harder it will get. This applies to all the possible causes mentioned above: the more you worry, the more anxious you get and the less energy you then have to really face up to your problems. By the time you need to overcome them, you are exhausted.

Second, focus on the HERE and the NOW. The more time you spend either in the past or in the future...

- ✓ The less time you have to focus on the problem at hand;
- ✓ The less energy you have when you finally decide to tackle the situation in front of you;
- ✓ The less aware you are of the real circumstances around you and the less resources you are then able to perceive and find; and
- ✓ The less you learn for future, similar situations.

In order to be in the here and the now, you need to make the conscious effort to do so. You need to fight the habit that drives you away into the past or the future. A good tool to use is any form of mindfulness:

- ✓ Focusing on one object around you and assessing it using your 5 senses: smell, touch, taste, hearing and sight;
- ✓ Focusing on feeling your ten toes without actually moving them;
- ✓ Engaging on any type of activity by totally submerging yourself in it through your 5 senses.

Another important tool to be used is drastically stopping whatever you are doing and doing just the opposite or something completely different. For instance, if you're sitting and you suddenly realize you're ruminating or getting carried away into your mind, stand up and start moving. Or, if you're walking, just sit down anywhere or start dancing. Changing our actions forces us to be in the here and the now.

Third, use the Kaizen technique. We often feel overwhelmed, as was already discussed above, when there's too much on our plate. We have important goals to reach and those feel unreachable. Kaizen implies reducing our goals to more manageable steps and taking those steps, one by one. So, if you for instance, need to exercise because the doctor told you to, running or cycling for one hour everyday might sound like an impossible task. Applying this Japanese technique, you would start by only doing it for 5 minutes the first day and celebrating achieving that little milestone. The second day you would do it for just 10 minutes, then celebrate it, and so on until reaching the desired 60 minutes. Celebrating the small steps is a fundamental part of the process because it helps us change our beliefs and boosts our self-esteem.

Fourth, identify and question the beliefs that make you doubt yourself. In order to do this, I usually recommend using a "self-talk diary," a notebook (or recording system) in which to note down any negative or critical self-talk we catch ourselves using. All those messages to ourselves hide our deepest beliefs. An example would be you telling yourself... 'I will never get the promotion because nobody likes me,' which is another way of telling yourself that you're not likeable or worthy. Identify all the labels you give yourself in order to understand why your self-esteem is so low. Those are the messages you keep on telling yourself. Are you surprised you feel insecure? Do this for at least a couple of weeks.

Once you identify your beliefs (through those labels and messages), ask yourself wether they empower you or limit you and if you wish to keep them. If you decide to let them go, you will need to find a replacement, as no belief can be simply erased. In order to find a replacement, look for a message that cancels the previous one and start repeating it to yourself. There is one important rule here: the new message can not be the opposite of the previous one, because your brain will just not believe it. It needs to be one that partially cancels it, opening a new avenue for you. Using the same example as before, you might have been telling yourself that you're not likeable. Your new message could be something like, "some people like me," or "I sometimes like myself," or even, "there's a lot in me to be liked." Once you repeat it often enough, you might start feeling it come true. At that moment, celebrate the feeling. The more you do this, the easier it will be for you to start accepting the new belief and replacing the old one. Warning: question and change only one belief at a time and don't start on a second one until having worked on the first one for at least two weeks. Questioning too many beliefs simultaneously can lead to crises.

Fifth, use tool number 4 to also question yourself about your beliefs regarding competition and success. What do you believe about them? What are your expectations? What messages do you give yourself? Do they empower or limit you? Do you want to keep them?

Feeling overwhelmed is extremely prevalent and limiting. Use this information to start understanding and managing the reasons behind your feelings and things will quickly start changing for you. You have the power to change the way in which you interpret your circumstances and your reality. Start letting go of those limitations and take better control of your life.

Enjoy life... ALL of it,

SEVEN STEPS TO OVERCOMING OVERWHELM FOR CREATIVE, HIGHLY SENSITIVE, GIFTED PEOPLE

Do you find yourself feeling overwhelmed when life gets hectic-and that's much too often? Is creative expression essential to your sense of well-being? Is daily time alone crucial to your inner balance? Do you quickly get overwhelmed when there's lots of noise and activities going on? Do others frequently say that you're "too sensitive"? And do you sometimes feel like "a freak of nature" because of these things?

I have good news for you! Your creativity and sensitivity are gifts that the world sorely needs, not anomalies to be obliterated! It is possible to overcome your overwhelm (without losing your creativity or your sensitivity)! You can heal yourself from the effects of the things that overwhelms you, truly thrive instead of just survive, and yes, even achieve your creative, sensitive hopes and dreams.

Skeptical? Yes, I understand. I, too have been to all kinds of seminars, read books, listened to tapes and cd's, all of which purport to tell me how to heal, thrive and/or achieve, yet only overwhelm me or leave me feeling desert-dry and empty inside. For I, too and a Creative, Highly Sensitive Person. For many years, I have researched and developed tips, tools and techniques especially suited to help us Creative, Highly Sensitive People to heal, thrive AND achieve. When I find something new that seems useful, I try it; if it helps me without overwhelming me or leaving me dry or empty. And when it works for others on a small scale, I then distribute it on a larger scale. So, all of the tips and tools I share with you are ones that I have experienced personally, and have also been helpful to many others as well.

So what to do when we're overwhelmed? How do we Overcome Our Overwhelm?

The First Step is to recognize what is going on.

As elementary as this sounds, we often try to skip over it. It is essential that we admit that we're overwhelmed when that is what we're experiencing! We need to stop pretending that we're keeping up, doing fine, going along smoothly through life, when if fact, we are not! And what's more, I've found that it's helpful to recognize and admit it as soon as possible. How bad do things have to get before we acknowledge that they're not going well? Do we have to crash and burn, or can we allow ourselves to own up to the overwhelm without owning the overwhelm itself? In other words, when we recognize the truth of our situation, we can then begin to do something to change it. We can't do anything about feeling overwhelmed until we acknowledge it!

Then what? I have found three more steps in a process that work wonders to Overcome Overwhelm!

Step 2 is to de-escalate the overwhelm--to get the body back in balance.

Take some long, slow deep breaths, drink a glass or two of water, close the eyes for a few seconds at least; do one or as many of these, and similar things to restore inner balance, to get both of our feet back on the ground. If we have the luxury of more time, stretch some muscles, take a lavatory break, eat a small, healthy snack, walk around the block, do something playful, get in nature for a few minutes. Gratitude and humor can also be important to restore balance quickly.

Step 3 is to identify the source(s) of the overwhelm.

When we're overwhelmed, it's like our bodies' circuits have overloaded, and our central nervous system has shut down some of them. And just like we do in our homes when that happens, a good place to start is to check with our bodies, our minds, our souls, and our spirits. We check each "circuit" to see which one(s) are overloaded. For example, we check for too much noise, too much happening too fast, too many projects going at once (also much like too many programs open on a computer), multitasking in too many ways, inner aches or voids, nagging doubts or worries, responsibility without authority, unrelenting stress, continual dissatisfaction with some area of our lives, too much stress of any kind. It's important to identify all the stressors that are impacting us at that particular point in time. We don't do anything about them just yet, only identify them.

Step 4 is to unhook from the overwhelm.

Just like we do when our house circuits are overloaded, when we discover which circuit(s) are overloaded, we then search to find what can be unplugged or turned off to free up the circuits for what is essential. I have learned to ask myself, "If I could get only one thing done today, which one would it be?" I then unplug from everything else, and focus on only one thing. Other useful questions can also be: What can wait, and what cannot? What will make a difference five or ten years from now? What must be done first, before other steps can be taken? Many people find that making one or more mind-maps of their "circuits" can be especially helpful.

Step 5 is really the first step in importance: Identify what our lives are about; what is our mission, and our vision for our lives?

What makes it worthwhile to get out of bed in the morning? What is our destiny? Why are we here on earth? What are our unique gifts, and how are we going to use them to benefit others? What unique challenges have we faced with creativity and aplomb, (and yes, blood, sweat and tears, too!) and what have we learned (often at great cost in life, energy, soul & spirit) to us, that we could bless others if we would be humble enough to share (our mistakes, of course, which leads to) what we have learned?

Step 6 is to plan a pace and a way of living that builds in the essential elements that we need to live that mission and vision, AND stay out of overwhelm at the same time.

It is much easier, and is often tempting to live like a rabbit, hopping here and there, setting the stage for continual overwhelm, than to plod along like a boring turtle. Yet, turtles have lots to teach us about healing, thriving, and achieving. They teach us of slowing to the pace of completion. They teach us about pulling into our shells when we need a break. They teach us about giving a warning snap when our boundaries are threatened. They teach us about going with the ebbs and flows in life. They teach us to ground ourselves when we are disconnected from our inner selves, with gratitude, and solitude. They teach us that a slow, plodding (boring) pace may, in fact, be the easiest and best way to arrive at our desired (creative, sensitive) desired destination.

Step 7 is to build in borders, blank spaces in our lives.

We need time to breathe, to reflect, to step back from the day to day grind of life and take a break. We need a change of pace. We need to experience new places and faces, and no faces at all at times. We need off-time, down-time. We need this in small, frequent, daily or more, little bits of time, and longer, extended weeks or months. We need exciting times, up times, on times, when we are in flow, performing at our peak, and we need distinction between the on and off times.

HOW TO BE A POSITIVE PERSON

Positive, happy people do have an easier time in life, and bounce back from problems faster. There are always things you can do to increase your level of optimism, even if you can't change who you are. Whether you realize it or not, you are responsible for lifting your own feelings and no one else is responsible for making you feel better.

To become more positive:

> **Write down and visualize your goals:** this programs your brain to help you find the positive steps you can take to meet your goals. It will alert your brain to notice things and events that are related to your goal. You will automatically be more aware of certain events, opportunities and people who can be helpful. You'll also be more clear about what

you want, and this will sneak into your conversation and your general attitude, where others can pick up on it.

➢ **Ask politely for what you want:** The easiest way to get what you want is to make a pleasant request, and deliver it with a big smile and a warm look. Please is very important, and so is a gracious smile, eye contact, and a warm thank you when the request is met. If you make requests confidently, as if you expect to get a "yes," it ups the odds that you'll get one. "Please go to lunch with me" works better than "You wouldn't want to go to lunch, would you?"

➢ **Dress as if you feel special, and act that way:** The more you respect yourself, the more others will respect you. Make sure you present yourself well, dress and act the part.

> **Accept favors, gifts and compliments gracefully, with thanks. Don't worry about whether you deserve the compliment:** if someone says something nice, and you respond that you don't deserve it, you're effectively calling that person a liar; which is not charming at all. Gratitude for kindness begets more kindness. Nothing works better than a pleasant "thank you so much" to make the kind person feel appreciated, and wanting to give you more. You can also accept credit and still share credit with others: "Thank you so much; it was really Susan's idea." Accepts the compliment and shares the love.

> **Practice a new situation before you do it:** I recommend the "roll the tape" exercise: picture yourself taking some small risk, and watch the scene play out. "Re- roll the tape" several times, and go through the scene again. Practice some different responses and different approaches until you feel comfortable with it. Then, you can try it in the real world.

To enhance your positive experience, do the following steps before any new activity:

1. **Make a mental note of the possibilities:** Can you learn something there? Can you meet a new friend? Could it be fun? Will just getting out of the house and around new people feel good?

2. **Remind yourself of your goals:** You're going there to make new friends and to have fun or to learn.

3. **Review your positive personal qualities:** What do your friends like about you? What do you like about you? Your intelligence, your sense of humor, your style, your conversation skills? Are you a kind and caring person? Reminding yourself of these qualities means you will enter the event radiating that positive energy.

➢ **Change your thinking:** Everyone has running dialog in their heads, which can be negative and self-defeating, or positive and energizing. Your thoughts affect your mood, and how you relate to yourself can either lift or dampen your spirits. Neuronal activity in the brain activates hormones which are synonymous with feelings. One thing you can do is to monitor your self-talk: what do you say to yourself about the upcoming day, about mistakes, about your luck? If these messages are negative, changing them can indeed lift your spirits and your optimism. The good news is that you can choose to replace your negative monologue with something more positive.

Self-talk is the most powerful tool you have for turning your negative feelings to positive and your negative interactions with your partner to love. Your brain tends to repeat familiar things over and over, wearing the established neuronal pathways deeper and deeper. Repeating a mantra, an affirmation or a choice over and over creates new pathways, which eventually become automatic. The new thoughts will run through your head like the old thoughts did, or like a popular song you've heard over and over.

> **Make the best of who you are:** if you love silence, tend to be quiet, like quiet conversations and not big parties, this may be a genetic trait: your hearing, and nervous system may be more sensitive than someone else's, and this trait will not go away. You can, however, make the most of it, and learn that creating plenty of quiet in your life will make you a happier person. Quiet moments with your partner will be especially meaningful to you, and make you happy.

If, on the other hand, you're a party animal-social, enjoying noise and excitement, you can also use that as an asset. You will bring the party to your relationships and music and activity will lift your spirits.

➢ **Take charge of your negative thoughts:** (that's one thing totally in your control) and turn them around; argue with them, fight them off, wrestle with them. Put energy into it. Let go of whatever you can't control, such as other people, life's events, loss, disappointment. Stop trying to change what won't change, accept what is, let it be and live life as it is. Yes, I know it's easier said than done, but once you get a handle on it, life itself is easier. Fretting about what you can't control is an endless, useless waste of energy you can use elsewhere.

Here are some things you can try that will help in making you more positive:

a. Make a note: Write positive comments to yourself on your daily calendar for jobs well done or any achievements you want to celebrate. Your partner will also appreciate little love notes or thank you notes left around to surprise and delight.

b. Look to your childhood: Use activities that felt like a celebration in your childhood: did your family toast a celebration with champagne or sparkling cider, a special dessert, a gathering of friends, or a thankful prayer? Create a celebration environment: use balloons, music, flowers, candles, or set your table with the best china. Work with your partner to incorporate both of your childhood celebration elements.

c. Use visible reminders: Surround yourself with visible evidence of your successes. Plant a commemorative rosebush or get a new houseplant to mark a job well done, or display photos of fun events, and sports or hobby trophies. It's a constant reminder that you appreciate yourself and your partner that you'll both feel daily.

d. Reward yourself and your friends: Go out for ice cream, high five each other, toast with champagne or ginger ale in fancy glasses, take a day off for just the two of you, and party every chance you get.

e. Try laughter: Find a way to laugh with your partner and others around you every day. Share jokes, funny memories, comedic movies and Internet jokes. It will lower your blood pressure, calm your pulse and generally help you release a lot of stress.

Gratitude

Gratitude is something that always helps remind us that life is not all bad. Every day I see the positive effects of getting my clients to focus on gratitude. The things we feel good about are easily taken for granted, so making sure you spend some of your time noticing what you're grateful for gives you a chance to register the good things in your life, reduce your stress and anxiety, and feel better about yourself, your relationship, and your life. While stress and anxiety cause the body to release adrenalin and testosterone, focusing on gratitude floods you with oxytocin, acetylcholine and other calming, relaxing agents. Hormones are emotions, emotions are hormones, so when you're flooded with happy hormones you'll feel good, and so will those around you.

    a. Daily thanks: Take some time each day to be thankful for each and every thing that comes your way. Do this silently, for yourself, not ostentatiously, to impress others. If you say a grace before meals, say it silently, and think about how fortunate you are. Hold hands with your partner or family and give thanks for your love.

b. Keep a gratitude list: For one week, list every good thing that comes your way- a funny e-mail, a phone call, a business success, a loving gesture, or a sweet moment with your partner. At the end of the week, you'll be astounded at how much you receive.

c. Thank your loved ones: Thanking your partner allows both of you to feel valued. Gratitude is powerful, and, used properly, a much greater motivator than demanding, criticizing, or nagging. Creative gratitude is the most powerful kind. It's easy to scope out what kind of thank you will be memorable for a particular person, when you're paying attention. Recognition is a powerful motivating factor, and a little gratitude can go a long way.

d. Counter negative thoughts: Whenever a negative thought comes to mind, counter it by giving thanks for something that is good in your life. Change your focus from what's wrong to what is right.

e. Count your blessings: Count everything you already have that you cherish. Consider beginning a gratitude journal, and noting all the positive things, beloved possessions, and tender moments you experience. Or, start a gratitude jar, and note down on scraps of paper all the positive things, beloved friends, favorite possessions, and tender moments you experience in your life and relationship, and store them in the jar. Then whenever you feel frustrated, down or discouraged, pull out a few papers and read them. You'll find that reminding yourself of all you have to be grateful for will cheer you up and help you remember that your life is a good one.

f. Get to know yourself: Just checking in with yourself on a daily basis, knowing how you feel and what you think about whatever is going on in your life will make you happier, and reduce your stress. Being kind to yourself and having a good relationship with you will make all your relationships with other people go more smoothly. Whether you realize it or not, the relationship you have with yourself sets the pattern for how you connect with your partner. By developing a nurturing way to relate to yourself, you create a personal experience of both giving and receiving love.

g. Know how to soothe yourself: Familiarity with your feelings helps you make appropriate choices in every phase of your life. When you know how you feel, you also know how to comfort yourself when you're stressed or tired. What makes you most comfortable? What soothes you? What helps you recharge? It can be anything from a bubble bath, a kick around in the park, a yoga session, or your favorite music to a long walk in the country, a good workout, a phone conversation with your best friend, or a nap. Make a list of your favorite "personal rechargers" and include simple things you can do cheaply (such as relax with a cup of tea and read a favorite book) and also things that are very special (such as a holliday or a massage or a facial). Keep the list where you can refer to it whenever you feel in need of a recharge, and make use of it often.

h. Maintain your happiness: Doing what you can to bring as much happiness as possible to yourself and others. Being happy is undeniably good for you; the endorphins it releases reduce stress and pain, and boost your health and immune system. Happiness makes you glad to be alive and pleasant to be around.

i. Set aside regular time for yourself: Me time is important for nurturing your relationship with yourself. It is proof that you care about yourself, just as when a partner spends time with you, you feel cared about. Take your time for you as seriously as your business appointments or time with your partner. It will help you stay on an even keel, and be a better partner.

j. Spend time with people you love: Being with people you care about and who care about you is a great way to affirm your value as a person, and to confirm that your life has meaning and purpose. Make sure you take good care of your friendships and your relationship. Knowing you are loved is a great way to take care of you. Emotional maintenance means thinking about emotional health and staying in touch with your feelings. When you focus on emotional self-care, you and your partner will find hope and energy are created, which gives you even more reason for gratitude.

HOW TO USE POSITIVE AFFIRMATIONS

Positive Affirmations, how do they work? What changes can I expect?

Affirmations are one of the tools you can use to radically change your life. There is nothing new age, mystic, trendy or fashionable about them. Affirmation is part of an ancient ' Secret', re-discovered and brought back to the limelight by TV. film and press, transforming with it several people into very wealthy gurus.

Affirmations have been around since man found the use of language and there is no secret ritual to use them. You can basically have anything you want! This tool, if used correctly, will help you change, grow, and heal yourself.

When you start the affirmations, give yourself at least a thirty day tryout period. Depending on the seriousness of the problem you may need more time and more affirmations to achieve your goals. Talk to your family and friends about your resolution to change and ask them for their support. If it is a radical change you are envisioning a life-coach will be very useful suggesting the best approach to use and to keep you motivated. This is a big step. Opening up to relatives and friends show your commitment to change and solidify your intentions.

Don't get discouraged, impatient or put off if nothing happens in a week or two. Just remember that you didn't become this way overnight. Affirmations can and will transform your life patterns and perception.

Affirmations support your positive thinking and together they form a very powerful and effective tool. They function as 'key words' of positive messages 'dictated' directly to the self.

You consciously connect and direct your positive thinking to areas of your life that you want to change or heal. It works as a reminder to the self, keeping positive messages at the forefront of consciousness. The benefits of affirmations are medically well established and really work.

On the other hand negative thoughts are just as powerful. So be aware of your negative thoughts as they are in essence self-destructive 'key words:' psychological mechanisms that make your life rotten.

First, let's check how aware you are of your thoughts. Do you regularly have more positive or more negative thoughts running through you mind?

Only you can honestly answer that. So get ready.

If your subconscious is throwing out lots of negative thoughts then you must do some 'brain-cleaning' before moving into the desired new positive affirmation mode.

This may be very familiar to you, as your mind swirls with thoughts like: "I don't like this, I like that, I feel great, I hate him/her, I am afraid of, I don't want them to see me like this, I am not sure about that, I feel rotten".

Your mind incessantly interprets your experiences as an internal dialogue. These thoughts are generated on a deep level by your beliefs which were formed and accumulated from the time you were born. We can't control most exterior events of our lives but we do control how we interpret and react to them.

We create our own reality.

When we change our interpretation a change takes place in our reality. So become aware of your thoughts. If you change your thinking, big changes will happen in your life. Take a minute to think about why you are reacting to something or someone.

Get in touch with yourself. Accept the fact that these thoughts may have helped you in the past but they are out of place now that you have chosen to accept only positive thoughts and positive living.

While doing the new affirmations your mind will let go of the negative messages even if you are not aware if it.

Watch out also for resistance within yourself. With certain affirmations you may question, "What in the heck" - "are you kidding?"

It is ok, it is an old habit that is about to be changed. You grew up and had these thoughts for almost all of your life. Now it is time to form a new habit and you need lots of practice.

Let's get started.

What would you like your life to be?

Think about it and write it down.

Fulfillment with your job, a happy family, better health, financial security?

Don't hold back, go for it.

For the beginners the easiest way is to choose and write down two or three things you want changed.

For example, if you feel unloved and financially strapped, one of your affirmations could be: " I am now ready to receive more love and wealth" and you may add "from the vast supply of the universe".

If you also wrote down 'low self-esteem' the affirmation could be: "I am an awesome man/woman and I feel good about myself".

Be creative, upfront and fearless. You are making a statement to yourself of your intentions.

Here are a few simple guidelines:

1- Present tense. Start all your affirmations in the present tense and have them already accomplished. You are telling your conscious mind that the affirmative action is taking place NOW and it is final. I AM HAPPY, I CHOOSE JOY, I HAVE CONFIDENCE. It is stronger and much more powerful than, I will be happy, or I am becoming happy, and so on.

2- How to phrase your affirmations. You can copy from an extensive list you'll find on the Internet, use the examples below or simply write it down in your own words. Do it as plainly or as poetically as you speak. " I am energetic and full of enthusiasm. I am safe, I am a prosperous man/woman. I attract positive people, I release my anger." Make copies of it and leave it around the house, car and your office desk. The more you are reminded of the positive affirmations the more your mind will accept the new concept you are bringing forth. You will create a new positive reality and the universal energy will do the rest to connect this good energy to other positive energies.

3- Positive means Positive. Your subconscious usually focuses on the verb and relates it to past experiences. If you have fears, phobias or whatever, be careful with your choice of words. If you are afraid and say I am not SCARED, it will register I

AM SCARED. The NOT was assimilated and ignored by your mind. Say instead I AM COURAGEOUS or I AM FEARLESS. Don't use affirmations that have a negative attachment. You can comfortably use I ACCEPT, I CHOOSE, I DESERVE, I AM. I developed one affirmation to counteract the negative thought that eventually peeks through, so I suggest you add it to the batch, "I ACCEPT ONLY THE GOOD AND THE POSITIVE."

Starting as you wake up, say the affirmations out loud or in your head five times. Repeat the same process three to four more times during the day, the last one just before going to bed.

I suggest you end the affirmation session with a thank you note. Gratitude will reinforce and validate the affirmations. Thank God, a Spirit, the Force, the Universe or whatever you believe and feel comfortable with.

Visualize your affirmations with feelings and emotion. See yourself exactly as you are stating. It will add an extra psychological dimension and have a much deeper impact on your mind. Using this method of visualization early in the morning and at night will make your affirmations much more successful.

You can use affirmations to help build self-confidence, self-esteem, self-improvement and personal growth. It can also help conquer your fears and anger management. Affirmations have been successfully used to relieve anxiety and depression and are an excellent tool for weight control.

Here are a few examples of affirmations by topics:

Love

- "I am ready to love and to be loved"

- "I am surrounded by love"

- "I love and accept myself exactly as I am"

- "The love I give out returns to me multiplied"

- "I am a loving, beautiful creative person and this is reflected in my relationships with others"

- " I am now ready to receive more love, support and wealth from the vast supply of the universe"

- "I see the beauty in my surroundings and I radiate joy and love"

Wealth

- "I deserve all that is good and prosperous in my life"

- "Money flows to me from expected and unexpected sources"

- "I deserve to collect all the wealth and the rich rewards of my success"

- "My income is constantly increasing"

- "I am well, I prosper, I am successful and I am free"

- "Abundance, like a river flows in my life"

- "I allow all the immense wealth and goodness of the universe to easily flow into myself"

Self-esteem - personal

- "I now have the power to bring about all the positive changes in my life I desire"

- "I am protected, guided, and connected with the highest good at all times"

- "My personality is radiant with success, beauty and happiness"

- "I am an awesome man/woman and I feel good about myself"

- "I am at peace with my choices and what life throws in my path"

- "I recognize and honor my talents, abilities, and skills"

- "I choose to live my life the way that makes me happy"

- "I am positively changing my life now, for the better in every possible way.

Have a great journey

PART THREE

SELF HEALING AND CONFIDENCE

What is hypnosis?

Contrary to what we might think, hypnosis is not what we may have seen in our favorite movies. You don't need a stuffy psychiatrist in an English looking sport-coat swinging a golden pocket watch back and forth in front of your face. Nor does it require a fast talking evangelist style person on a stage to put you into some kind of catatonic trance and then snap his fingers and make you quack like a duck. Those things are great for movies but in reality, thankfully, it's a little more subtle and simple.

Hypnosis is simply the use of common relaxation techniques to enter a very deeply relaxed state. That's it. There's really nothing magical or complex about it. Also, while practicing and studying the arts and techniques of hypnosis can certainly help you to achieve this relaxed state faster and more effectively, you don't need a degree or certification to be able to do it. If I had a penny for every program out there offering certificates for hypnotherapy, needless to say, I'd have a lot of pennies! We'll get to some techniques you can use to practice this yourself in a moment.

Why use hypnosis for building confidence?

As I mentioned before, during hypnosis, you enter a deeply relaxed state. In this state, you are able to access your unconscious or subconscious mind much more effectively. Because of this, certain repetitive suggestions can powerfully affect the deep parts of your mind where you core feelings and thoughts reside. Once you are able to access your subconscious mind, often you can purge many of the stale negative thoughts that are stagnating there and replace them with positive and more helpful ideas or thoughts by using hypnotic suggestions. Several programs out there have been using these techniques quite effectively to help people achieve many forms of personal growth.

This works for building confidence the same way it might work for improving your positive outlook, combating depression, fighting stress, overcoming addiction, self-esteem issues or anything else that is significantly affected by our subconscious thoughts. Using this technique can also help you eliminate self-doubt and destructive negative inner dialog and thus improve your self-confidence indirectly. Achieving a more positive idea of self can improve many different aspects of your life and for some people it will prove to be almost vital for any kind of success and happiness.

What not to do...

You may not realize this but your likely perform negative self-hypnosis on yourself on a regular basis. Most of us do. We have bad habits such as pessimism (often sold as realism,) sarcasm, cynicism and simply fearing and dwelling on the worst case scenarios in our lives.

We develop these habits into deeply rooted patterns and conduct very repetitive inner dialogs of negativity. These subtle but frequent negative suggestions begin to filter down into our subconscious mind and get comfortable there. It just feels safer to expect the worst. This is a self-defense mechanism attempting to protect us from disappointment. Ignorantly, our mind feels that if it expects failure, it won't be hurt if that failure becomes reality. In truth, your mind will seek that safety and begin to manifest failure in your life. Your mind begins to associate that feeling of safety with failure. It prefers it to the pressure and stress of facing scary situations.

Like anything important, our minds need proper management. Another example of common self-hypnosis that we do frequently is daydreaming. When we daydream our negative habits and dialogs are allowed to sink deeper into our core mentality. Additionally we often daydream specifically about negative outcomes that we fear. When we do this, we are actively planting the seeds of failure. We are getting our brains more familiar and thus more comfortable with failure than success. If there were any singularly great reason to eliminate negative thought habits, this would be it. Stopping this alone can work wonders for your self-confidence and for your life in general.

So, knowing how easily we slip into the practice of self-hypnosis to program bad stuff into our minds, it should be obvious at this point that the first step should be to recognize the potential that this has when we apply it with purpose, to program positive thought instead.

If you are thinking that this all sounds a bit hokey, don't worry. Skepticism is natural and sometimes it is good to think critically and screen information as we receive it. Just don't let that skepticism rule your life. Don't let it prevent you from learning more, practicing it and seeing for yourself what works and what doesn't.

So how do I do it?

Let's look at some techniques and methods of self-hypnosis.

This is one that seems to work well for me. First, find a quiet comfortable place. You want to be alone and remove any distractions. It is also helpful if possible to do this when you don't have any pressing imminent engagements or tasks waiting for your attention. If you feel rushed, it will be exponentially more difficult.

Now settle in and sit comfortably. Close your eyes and begin to take deep breaths and exhale them slowly. Get into a steady rhythm of deep breaths and focus your mind on nothing but your breathing. Once you get into a comfortable rhythm, imagine that you are inhaling the positive energy and positive thoughts that you need and exhaling the negative ones. Visualize it. Try to keep this rhythm going for about 5 minutes. Your body and mind should begin to relax substantially.

Visualize your goals.

Once you notice that you have entered a much more relaxed state, begin to imagine your goals. Imagine what it will be like when you are actively and successfully achieving these goals. Again, visualize it. Put yourself into this vision completely and notice everything about it. Use all of your senses to explore this imaginary situation. How does it feel? How does it look? Where are you? What objects are there? How does the room smell? What taste is in your mouth? What sounds are around you? Etc.

Now imagine that you have already achieved that goal in the same way, once again using all of your senses to fully immerse yourself in the moment. Remember to continue your deep slow breathing throughout this entire process. See what it feels like to have accomplished your greatest goals. What does it allow you to do? How do you feel about yourself? How has it changed you? How do people react and respond to you now that you have proven your success?

When you feel that you have explored this fully enough, have filled yourself with positive thought and have entered a deeply relaxed state, you are ready to come back. Begin to count your breaths from one to ten. With each count, you become more awake and aware of what is around you. When you get to ten, open your eyes. You are finished.

You should feel more refreshed, relaxed and positive now. Unfortunately, these effects will not last forever. There is more work to be done. You have to undo years of negative seed planting. The good news is that you now have a massive new tool to plow up that old soil, fertilize it and plant a new crop. You can use this on a smaller scale to conquer your fears of specific tasks as well. This allows you to use this technique for building confidence. For instance, if you need to give a speech or presentation, you would visualize yourself completing it successfully while you are in your relaxed state. Combine this technique with your goal setting processes in order to expand your comfort zones and build your confidence in steps. You can also use positive affirmations during this relaxed state in order to apply it further and more specifically for building confidence.

Get into a routine and do this as often as possible. It will then begin to get easier. As it becomes a regular part of your life, you will find that it will begin to have much more permanent effects.

Another Hypnosis Technique

This technique is also common. It is similar to the previous method but slightly different and a little briefer. For this procedure, you will again find a quite place with no distractions but this time you want to have some kind of relaxing sound to focus on. The sounds of ocean waves, a ticking clock, wind or rain are some examples that work well. This time, focus on one goal alone. It can be big or small. Recite this goal aloud and memorize the way it sounds. Now focus on a single object in the room. Some say to use something above eye level but I've found that it also works with other objects so that part is up to you. As you focus on your object, begin taking the slow deep breaths just like in the previous method. Feel your mind and body begin relax. Then close your eyes and slowly shift your focus to the relaxing sound.

Continue this breathing and focus on the sound until you are able to enter the relaxed state. Once there, imagine a beautiful staircase. The staircase symbolizes your journey. At the top of this staircase is your one goal (the oasis of your achievement). There is nothing else here. There's just you, your staircase and your goal at the top that awaits your imminent arrival. Now imagine that you begin to climb. Visualize it. You take one step at a time and with each step, you leave more of your worries, doubts, fears and inhibitions behind. As you shed this unwanted weight, you become lighter and each step becomes easier. Continue until you reach the final step. Here you will pause and you will repeat your goal to yourself several times as you stand on the brink of your accomplishment. Now imagine taking that last step and standing atop the stairs amidst your glory. Slowly open your eyes. The session is complete.

Over time, with enough practice, your mind begins to believe in the ease with which you are making your way steadily toward your accomplishments in life. Doubts begin to slip away and your positive mind begins to work for you rather than against.

Here is another one.

Like both methods above, find a quite place with no disturbances and ensure that you are free of any pressing worry. Sit comfortably and this time you will breathe naturally. Close your eyes. You will focus on the relaxing of each muscle group beginning with your feet and working your way up all the way to your face. As you do this, allow you're self to get into a relaxed but natural breathing rhythm. Do this until you feel yourself become relaxed.

Now begin to imagine all of the things in your life that you are proud of and happy about. Consider any positive achievement that you can think of.

Imagine creating a huge picture of all of these successful accomplishments; a mural of sorts. This picture is vibrant and alive with sounds, voices, smells and tastes. You will now imagine and visualize your self stepping into this picture. In here, you are powerful, confident and unstoppable. This is the world of you at your best. You step into it boldly and as you enter the image, anchor your arrival with a powerful action or word of your choice. Make it strong or otherwise profound and say it to yourself in your mind. For example, you can use a statement such as "I am here!" or "I have arrived!" or you can simply snap your fingers, press your forefinger to your thumb or drive your fist into your palm. Do this to announce your arrival into your world of success. Let it be known that you are here and this place is yours. As you arrive, open your eyes. You are there and there is here. Not to sound like Dr. Suess but you are done. The idea is that this place and the real world are actually the same place and you can get there through this mental image using your anchor action.

Practice this until those anchor words or actions become strongly associated with confidently stepping into that image amongst your greatest accomplishments and owning it. The anchor action will signal that you are entering this place in your mind and you mind will begin to remember it.

With enough practice, you will be able to take yourself there and trigger this mental image by using your anchor action alone. Eventually you will be able to call up this powerful confident feeling on command and use it to help build your confidence any time you need it.

These are just a few of the more common techniques for self-hypnosis. They can be used to help you in numerous positive ways including building confidence. Try them and practice them and you will find results.

GET YOUR MIND RIGHT, BEGIN BUILDING SELF CONFIDENCE

So how do you prepare yourself to begin building self confidence?

Do you lack self confidence? First you need to recognize and fully understand the problem and take action to seek a solution. Next, you must begin to educate yourself. This is the step that lasts forever. To truly achieve progress, we must never stop learning.

One important thing to understand is that building self confidence is a process. It won't happen overnight but you can begin to see and feel results as soon as you start consistently working at it. The good news is that building self confidence is something that can easily be achieved with a little knowledge and some persistent effort.

As you begin to practice what you learn, and start building self confidence you will also begin to create more successes in your life. These successes will begin to compound the growth of your confidence itself. The result is a snowball effect that helps you learn how to be confident even faster than expected. Confidence creates confidence! Also once your self esteem gets repeatedly proven to you through the positive results that you witness in your life, your doubts will begin to recede into distant memory and disappear permanently.

The best way to approach building self confidence is to take the process in steps and the first step for any worthwhile endeavor should always be to get prepared.

- Get Prepared

To get prepared, you need to clearly recognize where you are and where you want to be. Only then can you create an effective plan to get there. You know where you stand in regards to self confidence.

You are aware of the types of situations that you can handle comfortably and the types of situations that you have difficulty with. Reflect on this for a moment and try to get a clear understanding of where you are right now with regard to your path to self confidence.

Now consider where you would like to be. Imagery is a powerful mental tool. Visualize yourself doing the things that currently make you uncomfortable. When you do this, picture yourself doing these things with ease, completely relaxed internally as if it were something that you had mastered and completed hundreds of times. If your mind can think it, it can achieve it. Now you have a clear picture of where you are and of something that you want to accomplish. File these mental pictures away or write them down, this is your motivation and you can return to it whenever you need to.

- Getting Your Mind Right

The next step to get your self prepared is to get into the proper mindset. You must believe that your goals are possible before you can reasonably commit yourself to them. If this is difficult for you, just remember to use consistent rational thought. If you think about this goal rationally, it becomes clearer that it is not only possible but probable that you can achieve it. These practices for building self confidence have been tried, tested and proven over many years and by hundreds of thousands of people before you and I. Humanity has had plenty of time and test cases to sort out what works and what doesn't by now. Rest assured that the information is out there and that what you desire is indeed quite possible. Eliminate any and all doubt about that right now. Accept it rationally and move on.

- Stop Defeating Yourself

Another important part of your mindset is to make sure that you stop working against yourself. We tend to pick up bad habits that perpetuate negativity in our minds. Make a conscious effort to remove self defeating thoughts and to stop saying anything that puts you down. They call these bad habits "self defeating" for a reason. That is exactly what they do! You've heard it many times "think positive", and you will continue to hear it if you ask people who know about how to be confident. Stay positive, stay focused and take baby steps.

- Examine your Strengths and Evaluate them Rationally

The best way to begin to recognize your strengths is to take some time and think back over your entire life. Starting as early as childhood if you want, find memories of each significant accomplishment in your life. Regardless of who you are, I promise that there will be many. Don't down-play anything. If you felt good about it, it matters.

Write it down. If you won a race in 3rd year primary and you remember the great feeling you had afterward, include it. You got the job out of 5 people that were interviewed? Include it. Compile a list. This will be something that you will refer to often (at least weekly) to remind you that you are actually quite capable of success. Focus on and highlight the ones that are the most important to you.

- Analyze your List

Now look at the list and think of it in terms of the things that you are currently comfortable with and the things that still make you uncomfortable. Are you able to see any trends? You should begin to see where your strengths lie. What are the things that you are good at? Write these ideas down as well. We all need to be acutely aware of our strengths when we set out to accomplish any significant goal.

- Develop a Plan

Another crucial piece of the process is the development of a tangible and clearly defined plan. This will help you measure and bear witness to the progress you make which will in turn reaffirm your belief that your efforts are paying off. By following a plan, you will learn how to be confident systematically and develop strong habits.

The plan should outline your goals. Start by brainstorming a list of things that you feel that you could not handle comfortably but that you hope to be able to handle with ease in the future. These are your specific goals. Include any accomplishment, even the ones that seem insignificant. For instance, I used to feel a little awkward when asking strangers for directions or help. I wanted to be able to approach and speak to anyone with confidence and so I would add this to my list. Don't be afraid to include the tough ones as well like asking for a promotion, giving a speech to a room full of 1000 people or asking the girl or guy down the hall out for dinner. Now put them in order from easiest to most difficult and focus on accomplishing each one before moving on to another.

Each small accomplishment will earn you some measure of improved self confidence that will help you to approach and achieve the next. Each accomplishment is a building block towards building self confidence.

This is "Textbook" Goal Setting

You will move through these accomplishments from easiest to hardest over time and each time you achieve one, just like accomplishing any goal, you will reward yourself by knowing forever that you can do this. These small triumphs will never go away. They are stepping stones along your path. Every time you move forward to another goal, consider how to apply your strengths to the situation to make it easier. "Work smart not hard" still applies whenever possible. Work on each step until it becomes as comfortable as an old hat. To this day, I still sometimes find myself asking people whom I don't know for directions or assistance, just to talk to them!! The things that we practice become habit.

Have you ever heard the phrase "fake it until you make it?" The idea behind it is simple and lends itself well to building self confidence. By practicing something enough and putting yourself out there, you will begin to incorporate these activities into your life in such a way that they become habit. They become easy. They begin to define you. To a significant degree, you are what you do. Once you realize this concept fully, you begin to see that you truly can become anything that you want to be. You take action and begin to define ourselves. You are seeking information right now which tells me that you are already practicing this concept whether you knew it or not. You are taking action to define or redefine yourself into someone with greater confidence. In a way, you are in fact learning how to be confident right now simply by taking action!

- Make a Commitment to Yourself

As you move forward in your learning and begin to progress toward building your self confidence, you will undoubtedly run into some stumbling blocks. There will always be some small desire to quit, give up or avoid. Just remember that taking the easy path is akin to hiding from challenge and works to break down your confidence rather than build it up. When possible, remain committed to your personal growth and push through challenges. The best part is, even if you fail, you will still gain confidence because you stood and faced the situation. You tried! There is significant courage to be found by simply facing the fear or doubt and making an attempt. If it doesn't kill you, it will make you stronger. If it might kill you, then by all means reconsider!

- Building Self Confidence Relies on Rational Thought

You will likely find that self doubt will always try to creep in. But you will be looking for it. Learn to recognize it for what it is each time it happens. When these doubts present themselves in your mind, all you really have to do is back up and truly and objectively examine the situation. Is it really possible to do this? Do people do this sort of thing all the time?

If so, then yes, it's quite likely that you can learn and do it as well. If on the other hand, you doubt something because of a rational objection, it is also quite possible that a significant challenge lies there and the situation may warrant further evaluation, a new plan or acceptance that it is an unlikely goal. If you are 50 years old and you haven't been in the Air Force or gone to college, becoming an astronaut might be a little bit out of reach, or perhaps the path would be so challenging that the means may not justify the end result.

For instance, at a certain time in a colleagues' life, he was determined to go to medical school and become a doctor. He was a great student, already had a bachelors degree and many of the prerequisite courses completed. However, he was 35 and also had 3 children and no income. He started out determined and confident but eventually doubts about this journey began to surface.

Careful examination told him that remaining dedicated and confident might get him pretty far and friends and family would help as much as they could but, 4-5 years of borrowing money and surviving with no income before being able to work again might prove to be more strife than it was worth. Trying to handle that while completing one of the most academically rigorous career paths in existence might not even be healthy. He simply did not have a realistic and maintainable plan that suited his current situation. Careful thought revealed that his motivation was based heavily on money and prestige which might be bad reasons to drag his family through such difficulties.

These realizations finally brought him around to reconsidering this career path as a viable option. The moral of this is that not all doubts are irrational and based on fear but many of them are. Be realistic when evaluating your doubts as well as your goals. As you continue to learn how to be confident, you will also learn how to better evaluate your goals and fears.

Hopefully some of these concepts will help you be better prepared as you continue along the path of building self confidence. Take this advice into consideration and prepare yourself mentally as you continue your efforts to learn how to be confident in all aspects of your life. You will be more open and willing to accept any direction that you receive. Get prepared and begin to make your way toward a new and more confident you.

So what do I do now?

Now you have a couple ideas about how to get your head in the right place but in order to send your self confidence levels to new heights, you'll need a plan and the willingness to follow it...

A BEGINNER'S GUIDE TO SELF HEALING MEDITATION

Are you stressed out with all that's going on? I'd be surprised to hear that you're not. Living in this quantum age means pushing the envelope to the max. It also means your life is full to the brim with issues, stresses, and struggles. With economic uncertainty abounding, people being laid off and the folks that still have jobs being required to do more, it's a wonder that anyone even knows how to relax.

Stress Is A Gateway for Disease

And as we all well know, stress is the gateway to all mental and emotional problems. Self-healing meditation is the best possible way to reduce stress and live a healthy and happy life.

One of the traditional methods of meditation involves focusing on your breath. Through this practice of focused breathing, your mind and body relax and you begin to experience an inner peace. The more focus and concentration, the better results you can achieve.

Meditation Provides Multiple Benefits

There are other benefits to meditation as well: higher degrees of concentration, clarity in the thinking process and an ability to handle what life throws at you with increasing ease.

Anyone can learn meditation, and though many think it's not for them, if you employ these simple tactics, you can increase the feeling of well-being in your life almost immediately in just a few minutes a day.

Basic Meditation Practices

The most basic form of meditation involves closing your eyes and counting as you breathe in and out. Be sure to breathe from your belly and not your chest. Expand your belly as you breathe. You do this by breathing in and mentally counting one-two-three-four-five-six, exhale one-two-three-four-five-six. Breathe in through your nose and out through your mouth.

As you practice this simple technique while focusing on your breathing, counting as you inhale and subsequently exhale, you'll notice that your awareness of the outside world diminishes. As you continue with this process, your entire body becomes oxygenated and your cells begin to buzz. Most people don't breathe properly throughout the day, so while this relaxes you, it also helps to oxygenate your entire body.

After you get the breathing part down, if you think positive thoughts during meditation, this will have an incredibly positive effect on your body as well. This is actually called Self-Healing Meditation which involves deep meditation practices. Through this practice, positive energy is passed throughout your body which will increase and aid the healing process. Even traditional NHS hospitals have taken to recommending this type of meditation for healing.

SELF-IMPROVEMENT - GOOD DAILY HABITS INCREASE MOTIVATION

One of the best ways to motivate yourself is to review your daily habits. Are they helping you or hindering you? If there are changes that you want for to make and you are having trouble accomplishing them it could well be that your habits are keeping you stuck.

Daily habits that keep you focused and moving forward are the key to motivation. We all have habits that will drain energy instead of creating energy for us. A good solution is to choose habits that you find energizing and which add to your sense of well-being. If you have little energy to accomplish things that matter to you then you may well want to review your daily habits. For instance, if you are eating foods that drain energy learning about nutrition and what foods are energizing may just be what you need.

Develop habits that give you pleasure when you accomplish them. If it matters to you that your bed is made every day then you are much more apt to put that on your daily habit list. You want habits that will keep you motivated and focused on growing your personal and/or business life.

The benefits of picking habits that you want to do are that your routine tasks will be quickly accomplished since you will be more focused, have more energy, and like the way you feel. Create habits that enhance who you are. Examples would be taking a daily walk, taking your vitamins, going to bed at a regular time, turning off the TV, reading, working in the garden, showing gratitude, or anything else that will make you feel good about the person you are.

Self-Mastery motivation comes from developing habits that matter to you and are part of the greater vision of what you want for yourself.

SELF EVOLUTION - LEARN HOW TO CHANGE YOUR LIFE BY CHANGING YOUR DAILY HABITS

What do you think about your life? Do you believe that, because of other people or unfavorable circumstances, you're not living the life you'd like to? If you believe that a dream is just a dream and it never will come true, you are wrong. You're just letting your life pass you by without even trying to give it a meaning. Finally, why are you living for?

We learn and acquire habits during all our life. Habits are those familiar and automated actions resulted from learning processes.

Any task or action we learn how to do and then perform repeatedly transforms into a habit. This is the mechanism through which we get used to do a lot of (good or bad!) things like: walking, cycling, reading, writing, driving a car, using the computer, smoking, watching TV, drinking coffee, hanging on forums or Facebook, etc.

Among all the actions we perform on a daily basis, good habits are those having favorable influence on our lives, while bad habits are the actions resulting in negative outcomes for us and for people close to us as well. Bad habits are usually called addictions.

But let me make a distinction here. Letting addictions aside, we can further split all our daily habits in habits which add in our personal development and habits which are just wasting our time.

Think a little bit of everything you do daily. What are you doing every morning, then during the time you spend at the office, and when you're back home in the evening?

Now ask yourself: will your life be different if you change any of your daily actions? If, instead of watching TV for two hours in the evening you read a book or learn something new on a subject that interest you, will anything change in your life? Or, if every morning you work out for a half an hour, will anything be different?

Have you ever thought about changing something in your life such as starting a new career, learning a foreign language or getting more fit?

Maybe you have even attempted to do new things or change old behavior patterns, but your enthusiasm didn't last too long. And you gave up.

It happened because habits are actions we make unconsciously. We just feel like we need to do a certain thing without asking ourselves why we have to or what is in it for us.

There are important changes in our lives that compel us to modify at least a part of our habits. This arrives for instance when we finish school and start working or when we get married, or leave our parents' home and move in our own place. In all these cases, we cut sharply the connection with an old familiar environment and have to adapt to a new one. When we feel at ease in our new environment, it means that the new habits are installed.

In most cases, this process takes place without us being aware of.

Now the question is: can we make consciously changes in our daily habits? How can we deliberately change our habits and overcome their resistance?

Changes in our daily habits are not only possible, but also advisable to be done when we decide to make bigger changes in our lives.

We firstly need to evaluate all the actions we are doing during the day, think about and decide which ones are good to be kept or even extended and which need to be replaced with better ones.

Secondly, through a step by step process, we are going to start making the desired changes.

It is very important to not overdue. Don't start with more than one habit and, at the beginning, my advice is to perform the new action for short time spans, then increase the time gradually. Once you have the first habit installed (it will probably take 1-2 months), introduce a new one. Making small steps every day is the best way to succeed.

Be prepared to overcome setbacks over time because habits are usually strong enough to not let us change them easily.

Make a plan and follow it, and be patient and persistent. Trust the method and be proactive.

In a few weeks you'll be proud of yourself, self-confident and ready to take on new challenges.

CONCLUSION

To a large extent, your happiness and your success in life is determined by the thoughts you hold in your subconscious mind. Positive affirmations are powerful statements that are used to build a positive internal dialog. By consistently repeating positive affirmations to yourself, you create positive subconscious thoughts. These new, positive, productive thoughts will replay automatically throughout your life. Each time they replay, they'll reinforce the new positive inner-image you have of yourself and your life in general. By replacing old, negative thinking with new, positive subconscious thoughts you'll be able to access the endless resources of positive energy you have within yourself. And you'll be able to create a new, positive reality for yourself.

When you use positive affirmations, let yourself really feel them. Fully experience each one. Enjoy them. Assume each affirmation to be true in your physical reality. Feel the positive emotions that are appropriate for this positive reality. This will help you make positive changes more quickly and automatically.

At the end of this report you'll find dozens of carefully chosen, time-tested, positive affirmations that will help get you started. Select those that you think will be most helpful. Write them down, carry them with you, and use them often. Get into the habit of saying them while you're doing routine things such as brushing your teeth or washing your hands.